ADVANCE PRAISE FOR *SOUL CALLING*

"Every coming to America is an act of defiance. But as Joel Pickford tells us—shows us—in this remarkable book, no journey to America quite matches the Hmong journey for sheer stubbornness. From the highlands of Laos they came, slash-and-burn farmers with no written language who would not easily give up their ways. From the 'stealing' of young brides to the sacrificing of animals to the growing of backyard opium, the Hmong have, indeed, perplexed us. With pen and lens, deftly tracing that headstrong journey, Pickford now shows us what is harder to see: that the Hmong, by clinging so obstinately to their past, have given us our own past."

—Mark Arax, author of *West of the West* and *The King of California*

"*Soul Calling* is a seminal and luminous work that compassionately documents the Hmong American experience in the Dorothea Lange tradition. Pickford's imagery is as lush as his prose, and his insights are deeply personal and thoroughly researched. I found myself fully immersed in fascination and delight."

—Cindy Wathen, coauthor of *Remembering Cesar: The Legacy of Cesar Chavez*

"Joel Pickford's photographs eloquently capture the story of the Hmong people as they struggle to make the transition from one culture to another. His images are moving and powerful, opening a window into a world few outsiders have ever seen. Reading Joel's first-hand account of his journey is also a very moving experience. Wonderful!"

—Cara Weston, photographer and coauthor of *Head in the Clouds*

"A spellbinding combination of photographs and text provide a fascinating account of Hmong life in Laos, the long and difficult journey to America, and the challenging resettlement of a group of recent refugees. Pickford's ability with both words and images is inspiring."

—Elizabeth Partridge, author of *Restless Spirit: The Life and Work of Dorothea Lange*

"'Fleeing the tiger to meet the lion,' the Hmong have become our neighbors. Joel Pickford takes us on a keenly observed, compassionate, and beautifully depicted five-year and eight-thousand-mile journey through the experiences of this diaspora people. By traveling from the new Hmong homeland in the Central Valley of California back to their American-bombed homeland of Laos, where some Hmong still live, Pickford allows us to see through gorgeous photos and words how so many souls might find themselves dislocated yet also called into a newly named and hopeful future in the United States. East-West encounters bristle on every page, as the artist meets his Hmong muse, Hmong musicians heal, and Hmong poets remember their history, much as ancient Greeks once did. This volume makes a substantial contribution not only as a work of art but also as an original piece of remarkably well-written—sometimes heartbreaking, other times humorous—scholarship in the field of diaspora studies."

—Honora Howell Chapman, coeditor of *A Companion to Josephus in His World*

"Joel Pickford's photographer's eye and poet's ear are exquisite. Through stunning pictures and evocative essays he traces his personal encounters with one of America's most recent immigrant groups, the Hmong. Pickford recreates his experience of their world with intelligence, humor, and fine sensitivity."

—Lillian Faderman, author of *I Begin My Life All Over: The Hmong and the American Immigrant Experience*

"Joel Pickford creates as many remarkable, lucid images with his prose as he does with his lens. He has achieved something rare in documentary photography, removing the perception of his own presence from the frame. And by so doing, he has become a compassionate and egalitarian witness to the previously invisible life of the Hmong."

—Christofer C. Dierdorff, portrait photographer, filmmaker, and director of *The Tapestry of Life*

SOUL
CALLING

SOUL
CALLING

A Photographic Journey through the Hmong Diaspora

TEXT AND PHOTOGRAPHS BY JOEL PICKFORD

Foreword by Kao Kalia Yang

Heyday, Berkeley, California

Heyday would like to thank the James Irvine Foundation for its support of Central Valley literature.

Library of Congress Cataloging-in-Publication Data
Pickford, Joel.
Soul calling : a photographic journey through the Hmong diaspora / Joel Pickford.
     p. cm.
 Includes bibliographical references.
 ISBN 978-1-59714-168-0 (hardcover : alk. paper)
1. Hmong Americans--California. 2. Hmong (Asian people)--United States. 3. Hmong (Asian people)--Laos--History--20th century.
4. Hmong (Asian people)--Thailand--History--20th century. I. Title.
F870.H55P53 2012
305.895972'073--dc22
                          2011011791
Cover Photo: *Qeej* player at the funeral for Hlaw Neng Thao Lee, Fresno, 2006. Photo by Joel Pickford.
Book Design: Lorraine Rath
Printed in China by Imago

Orders, inquiries, and correspondence should be addressed to:
     Heyday
     P.O. Box 9145, Berkeley, CA 94709
     (510) 549-3564, Fax (510) 549-1889
     www.heydaybooks.com

10   9   8   7   6   5   4   3   2   1

This book is dedicated with love to my three favorite children, Fentha, Bobby, and Sandy.

ປຶ້ມນີ້ຂໍ້ມອບໃຫ້ລູກທັງສາມ ທີ່ຮັກແພງ: ແຟນຕ້າ, ບອບບີ້, ແລະ ແຊນດີ້.

You are the future of Laos and the world.

ພວກລູກຄືອະນາຄົດຂອງປະເທດລາວ ແລະ ສຳລັບໂລກ.

CONTENTS

FOREWORD

Kao Kalia Yang

It has been twenty-four years since my family's long journey to America. For me, Laos is only alive in the stories my elders tell me. My father speaks of the mist over the mountains, of how the bellies of the clouds floated so low that a child could reach and touch them, floating in the mystical white fog of morning, feet on the earth. My grandmother told stories of how a tiger had chased her through the slice of bamboo leaves in a heavy jungle, how rivulets of Hmong blood seeped into the Laotian earth in the wake of the things that chased us. My memories of Thailand are those of a child. I see the open sewage canal that marked our side of the camp as the river of my youth, and the hungry dogs that prowled its dusty perimeters as the wild stallions of Southeast Asia. It is in America that I've lived the bulk of my life.

Those early years are a long-ago memory. I remember my cousins living in a two-bedroom down-stairs duplex along Maryland Avenue in St. Paul, Minnesota. Uncle Chue and Auntie had seven children then, five girls and two boys. The bedrooms were so tiny that my cousins couldn't all sleep in them. Auntie and Uncle slept on old twin mattresses placed side by side, with the two youngest in their arms at night. The three older girls shared a full-sized mattress in a room that was barely big enough for the saggy brown square of softness they rested on. The boys had to climb through a window to sleep on the porch. I remember how in the wintertime my boy cousins would wake up and crawl through that window into the dim living space with icicles in their hair and stiff, frozen lashes—even as they spent nights huddled beneath the mismatched quilts and comforters Auntie had gotten from the church basement. Each time I saw Kong and Sue with their spiky hair all stiff with cold, I wondered if I could break their frozen hair into chunks, crumble it with my small fingers and create black snow in the palms of my hands. From the distance of adulthood I can only marvel at the fortitude of young men and the imagination of a young girl…how we forgot to look at the faces of our mothers and fathers as we gazed upon one another.

Today I look at the photos by Joel Pickford and I see those faces from long ago—the young man and the young woman my mother and father must have been in the high mountains of Laos, babies on their backs, water pails balanced above trembling hips. I see my grandmother with her shaman's hood on, her flowery polyester shirt, facing the wall, lost in a trance, busy on a journey of saving us from despair of the spirit, loss of heart in the soul. I see my cousins and me playing kickball on cracked pavement, our green and blue flip-flops flying with the motions of youth. I see the walls of my aunts and uncles, my mother and father, myself: framed photos of us standing stiff and strong before painted murals of green. The world is resplendent in ill-represented perfection behind us, painted lines streaked with confidence, the scenes we've left behind, jungles we've never been to, American planes waiting, food spilling, men and women scrambling for flights that would free them from death. Joel Pickford has captured in the photos of this book the rich complexity of a people contending with war, with weapons, with hope and humanity.

As a first-generation Hmong American daughter, I am drawn to one photo of a grandma holding her grandson. The child wiggles as the old woman tries to hold him safe. Behind them, there is a taped-up fireplace. Beside them, an electric heater, unplugged. That grandma is mine. Her grandson is me. Many years have passed since I wiggled in my grandma's arms, her aged arms holding me safe. Far away and long ago, Grandma and I sat upon a manmade ledge, our backs to the hearth of a home lost in·the jungles of Laos. Beside us, there was a piece of American machinery, waiting to take us away. It is one photo of us in time, a photo that captures all of us for all of time.

As a young writer looking to document the strength and wisdom of our story, I cannot help but marvel at the photographer's eye on my people. He looks up at us. He looks directly at us. We cannot hide from the songs of the *qeej*, singing its melodies of loss. The faces of the dead man and the dead woman, the form of the dead child, all cold and closed to the world, capture the human heart when it can no longer beat for itself—when it must rely solely and exclusively on others to live on. We hear the call to come and eat away the hunger at tables full of white rice, delicately minced beef *laab*, the sweet of pumpkin soup, the steaming broth of fatty pork and dark wilted greens swimming across continents. Joel Pickford looks at the people, and in the photos they look back at him, eyes full of shyness, full of strength, grief and laughter glistening, hands and feet stilled and startling with exhaustion from the long journey we have taken.

The story Joel Pickford tells in *Soul Calling: A Photographic Journey through the Hmong Diaspora* is a story of how a people starved by war search for food in a nation whose history has never included them. This is a document of human experience across blue oceans and the expanse of generations. This is a portrait of how our elders bear scars so that we can carry armor in our hearts. The time for neglect and forgetting is through; may the Hmong spirit find its way on the long journey home to the places where our bodies are seen and our souls' cries heard.

Kao Kalia Yang is the author of the award-winning *The Latehomecomer: A Hmong Family Memoir* (Coffee House Press, 2008).

CALIFORNIA

The New Arrivals, 2004–2006

Plate 1

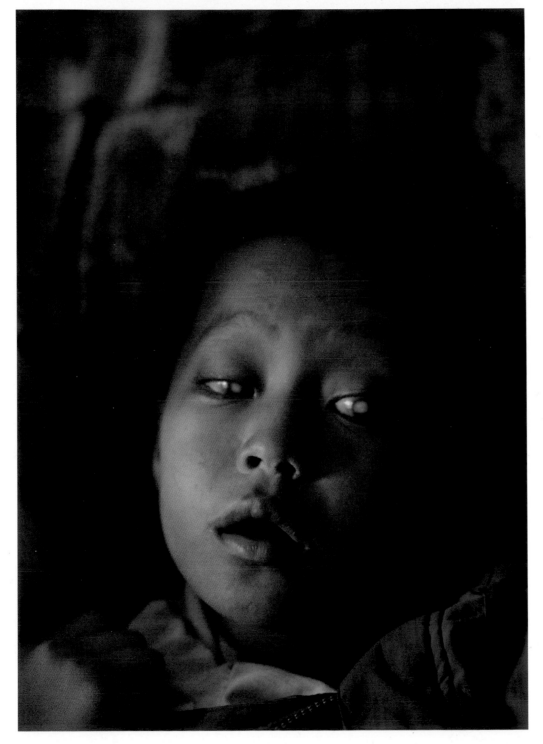

Plate 2

Plate 3

Plate 4

Plate 5

Plate 6

Plate 7

Plate 8

Plate 9

Plate 10

Plate 11

Plate 12

Plate 13

Plate 14

Plate 15

Plate 16

Plate 17

Plate 18

Plate 19

Plate 20

Plate 21

Plate 22

Plate 23

Plate 24

Plate 25

Plate 26

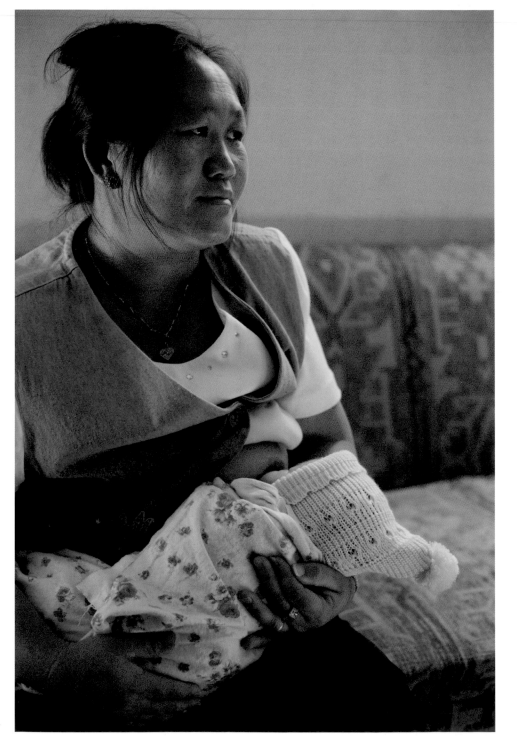

Plate 27

Plate 28

Plate 29

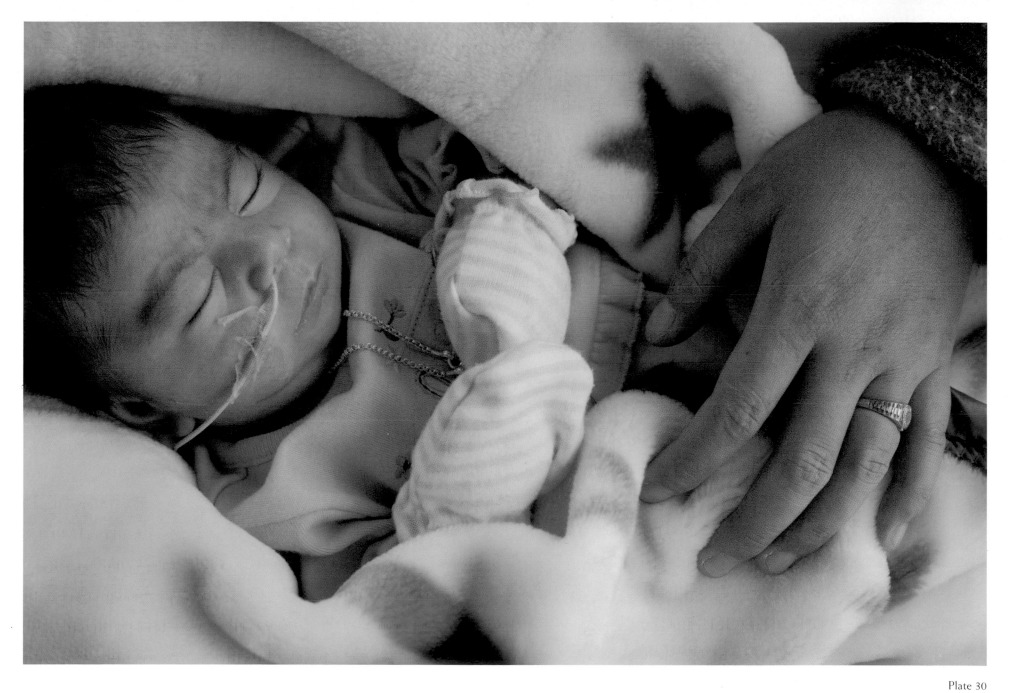

Plate 30

Plate 31

Plate 32

Plate 33

Plate 34

Hmong Americans

Plate 35

Plate 36

Plate 37

Plate 38

Plate 39

Plate 40

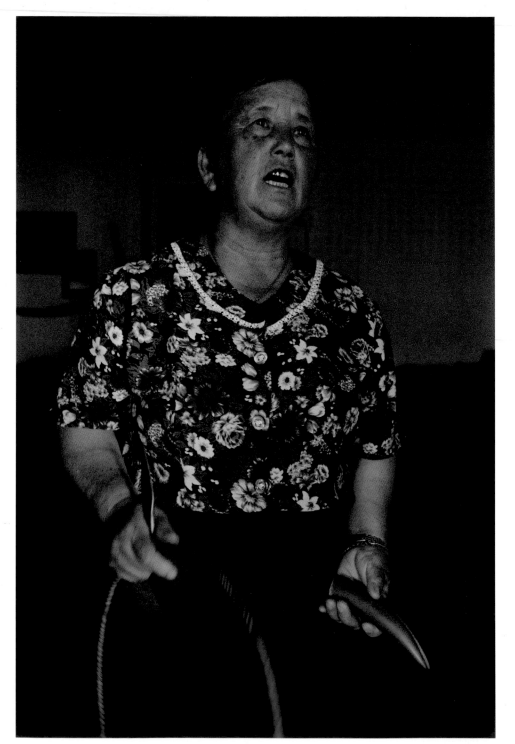

Plate 41

Plate 42

Plate 43

Plate 44

Plate 45

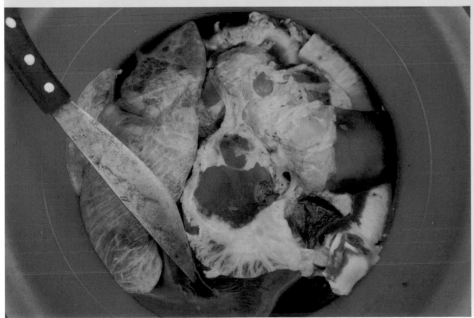

Plate 46

Plate 47

Plate 48

Plate 49

Plate 50

Plate 51

Plate 52

Plate 53

Plate 54

Plate 55

Plate 56

Plate 57

Plate 58

Plate 59

Plate 60

Plate 61

Plate 62

Plate 63

Plate 64

Plate 65

Plate 66

Plate 67

Plate 68

Plate 69

Plate 70

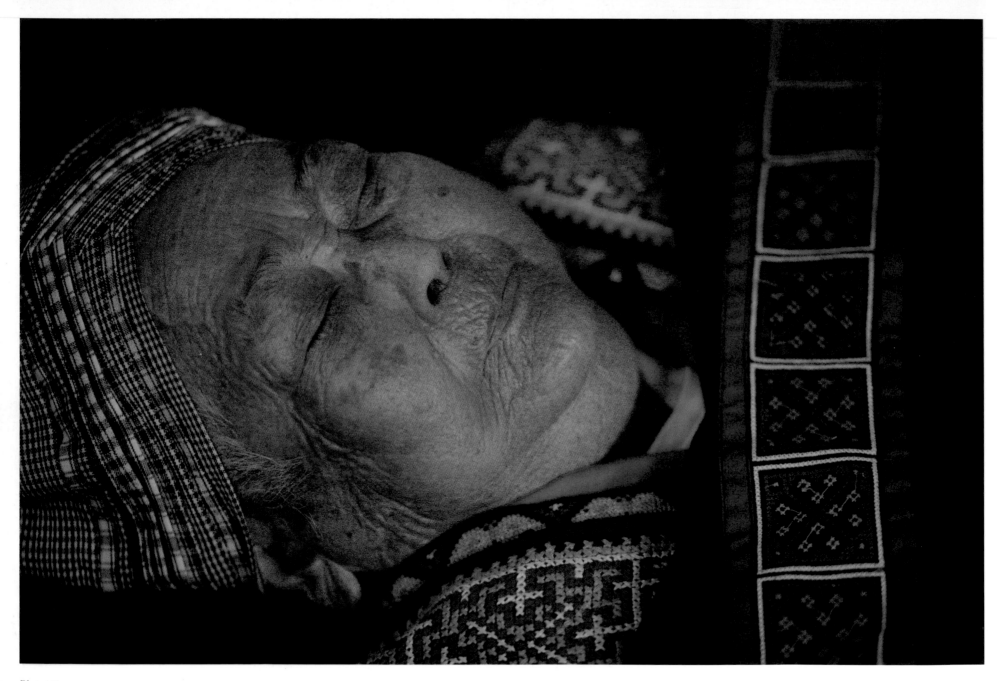

Plate 71

Plate 72

Plate 73

Plate 74

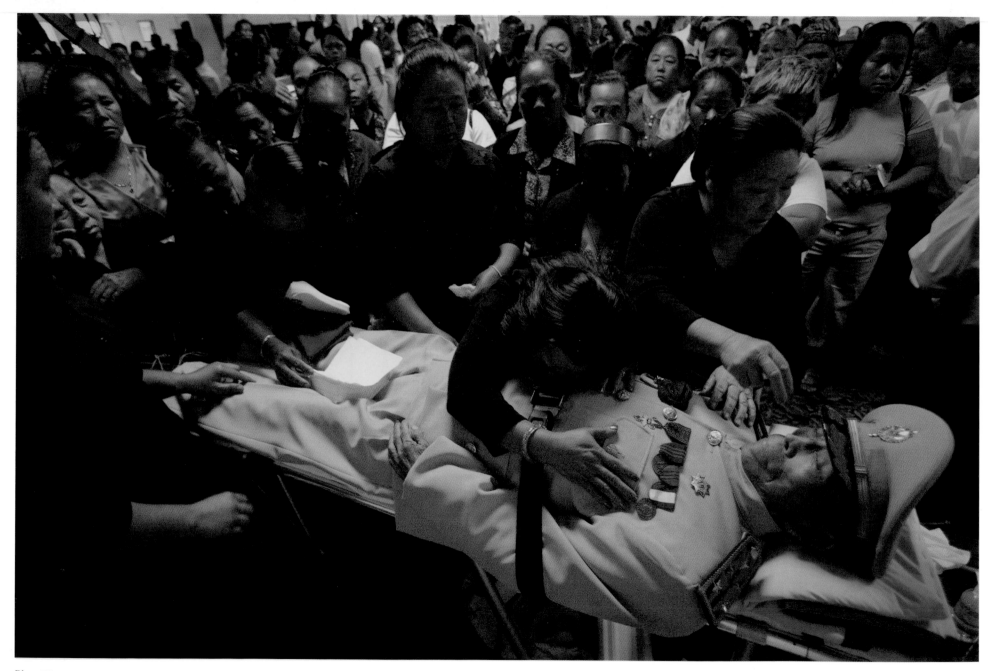

Plate 75

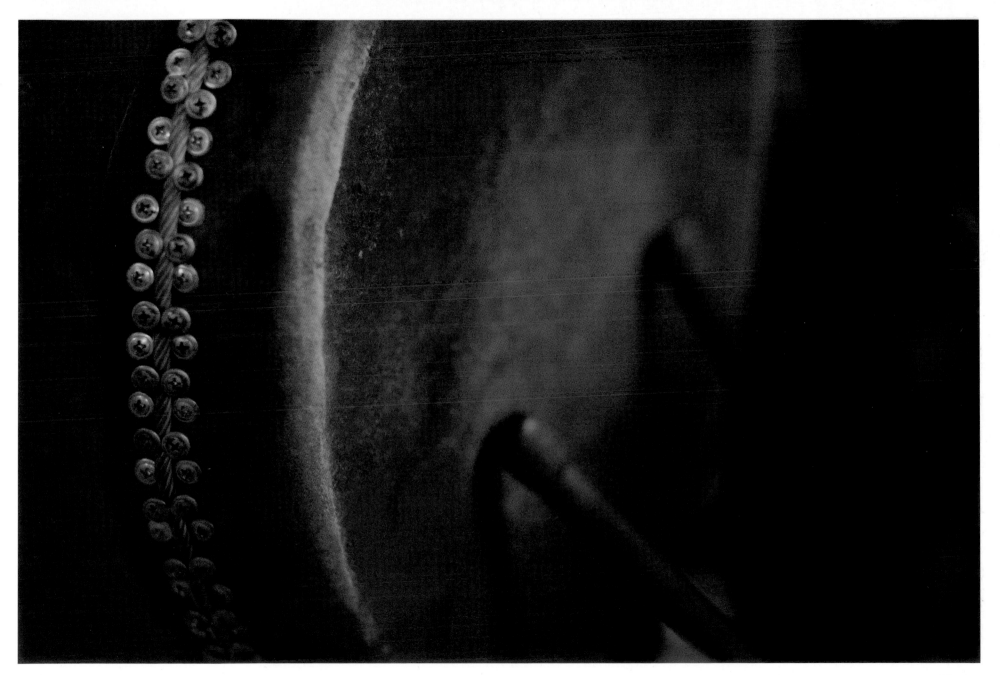

Plate 76

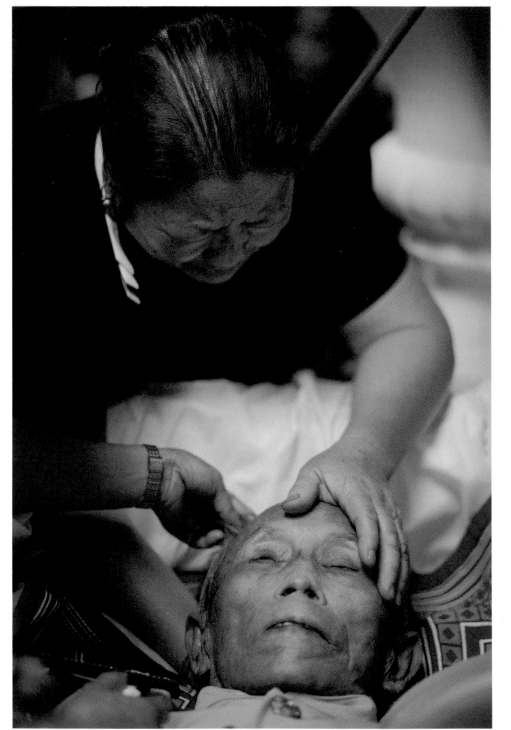

Plate 77

Plate 78

Plate 79

Plate 80

Plate 81

Plate 82

Plate 83

Plate 84

Plate 85

Plate 86

Plate 87

Plate 88

Plate 89

Plate 90

Plate 91

Plate 92

Plate 93

Plate 94

Plate 95

Plate 96

Plate 97

Plate 98

Plate 99

Plate 100

Plate 101

Plate 102

Plate 103

Plate 104

LOST AND FOUND

I arrive late to my first *hu plig*, awkwardly schlepping my bags of camera gear through the front door of an aging tract home in Southeast Fresno. I step over dozens of shoes that clutter the narrow entryway, adding my own conspicuously large runners to the jumble. The ceremony is already underway; two young women sit in the middle of the kitchen facing an altar covered in shiny gold paper and adorned with candles, Chinese herbs, water buffalo horns, incense, a black dagger, and an assortment of prescription medicine bottles. Behind them a dead pig lies belly-down on the floor, legs splayed out from its sides. Hours before the ceremony, in the predawn darkness, the pig was slaughtered, dipped in boiling water, and thoroughly scraped, leaving its naked skin the color of a newborn baby. A rope is tied loosely around the two women and then the pig, connecting their souls. An older, barefoot woman wearing a black hood slowly circles them, beating a gong and chanting in low, musical tones. Next, she picks up a large iron saber with a heavy blade and drags it behind her, tracing the same circle on the linoleum floor. Cradling a small bowl of water, rice, and a cooked egg in both hands, she positions herself behind the pig. She shouts an incantation, takes a mouthful of water from the bowl, and sprays the two women. After repeating this twice, she unties the women, who are now free to go.

The Hmong believe that if you become ill, experience bad luck, or suffer any kind of loss or hardship, it is because your soul has either wandered away from your body or been kidnapped by the *dab* ("da"), spirits that can be either good or bad depending on the circumstances. The purpose of a *hu plig* ("hoo plee"), or soul calling ceremony, is to return the soul to its owner. This involves the sacrifice of at least one animal, whose soul is bartered for the missing person's soul in the spirit world. The Hmong believe that pigs, chickens, and cows are always reincarnated as other pigs, chickens, and cows, so that their souls are merely borrowed for the ceremony. Like many American families, who pay someone else to kill a turkey for their Thanksgiving

family, he is caught in a void between two cultures he does not fully understand. Add the longstanding conflicts between Hmong and Lao to the mix and you have a volatile formula for domestic disaster.

In a *hu plig* ceremony like this one, the nature of the person's malady determines the size and quantity of the animals to be sacrificed. In this case the shaman has prescribed one pig and two chickens. After the two women leave the kitchen, the shaman sets a small pile of "spirit money" on fire and chants softly as it bursts into flame, then quickly disintegrates into ashes that fall to the floor. Fortunately, the battery in the ceiling-mounted smoke detector has long since died.

Next the shaman lowers the black hood all the way over her face and goes into a *ua neeb* ("wa neng"), or blind spirit trance, filled with intense musical chanting, wild exhortations, and talking in tongues. She beats out a steady rhythm with a pair of shrill finger bells. The high-energy ritual goes on for more than two hours as complacent family members casually saunter into the kitchen for a cold drink and then go back to the living room to watch Hmong bullfight videos from Laos. The intensity of the hooded shaman's trance builds as she begins jumping up and down on the bench, occasionally leaping to the floor and then back up again. Her sonorant vocalizing weaves a

dinner, the Hmong invite all of their relatives for a feast following the ceremony. No part of the animal is wasted.

The two young women for whom the *hu plig* is being performed are actually mother and daughter, separated in age by just fifteen years. They have recently emerged from an abusive relationship with the mother's ex-boyfriend, a Lao refugee who has lived half of his life in Thai camps and the other half in California. Estranged from his own long narrative, part memorized, part improvised, that takes her back through many generations of her family's history, revisiting the births, deaths, marriages, sorrows, and unpaid debts of her ancestors.

For the Hmong, the wooden bench in front of the altar represents a horse that the shaman rides into the spirit world to negotiate the return of the missing soul. The Hmong were once an equestrian people, riding small, sturdy horses with thick, bristled manes throughout the mountains of southern China and, later, northern Laos. Very few of these animals are found today in either country, as motorbikes, *sawngthaew,* and other conveyances have made them nearly obsolete.

After more than two hours of extreme physical and emotional exertion, the sweat-soaked shaman steps off her wooden horse, pulls off her black hood, mops her brow, and joins nearly fifty relatives for a feast of barbecued pork, chicken soup, rice, boiled vegetables, a congealed blood dish, and assorted cooked entrails. She examines the two chickens that her sons have killed and cooked during the ceremony, breaking into a satisfied smile. The translucent craniums and curved tongues of the boiled fowl are auspicious signs that the souls of the two women have come back. She gives the mother a new, secret name, in order to trick the *dab* into thinking that she is another person, so they will not steal her soul again.

PLAIN OF JARS

The flight from Vientiane to Xieng Khouang Province takes less than an hour, but in that brief interval, the fourteen-year history of Laos's Secret War unfolds outside the window of my plane. Almost immediately after takeoff, the Chinese-built twin-prop craft begins a steep climb over a range of jagged, dark green mountains creased with shadowed valleys. After about twenty minutes, the country's highest peak, Phou Bia (9,249 feet), looms on the horizon. From the right side of the plane I peer through the clouds, trying to catch a glimpse of Long Cheng, the deep cleft valley near the foot of Phou Bia still scarred with a landing strip the CIA built there in 1961. From this secret base, General Vang Pao commanded U.S.-trained Hmong ground forces in a slow but inevitable military retreat ending in 1975, when the country fell to North Vietnamese–supported Lao communists. Besides propping up the former royalist government, the strategic goal of the CIA operation was to disrupt North Vietnamese supply lines and communications along the tangled network of mountain roads and paths known as the Ho Chi Minh Trail.

Nearly every time I make this flight, my view of Long Cheng is obscured by clouds; only once did I get a spectacularly clear, if fleeting, view of the Secret Valley. Similarly, my efforts to understand what happened there four decades ago remain obscured by classified government documents and the polemical nature of books written on the subject. Read several histories of the Secret War and you will think you are reading about several different wars. Jane Hamilton-Merritt paints General Vang Pao as a gifted and courageous tactician who fought against the odds to save his people from communism. Alfred McCoy portrays him as a shrewd manipulator who used American air power to control the Laotian opium trade and coerce his people into fighting for the CIA, despite the near certainty of defeat. Roger Werner characterizes Vang Pao as an erratic and unpredictable commander, often working at cross purposes with an equally conflicted succession of CIA operatives. By now, most historians agree that the CIA used its private airline, Air America, to facilitate Laotian opium trafficking. The opium

General Vang Pao, 2008.

was refined into heroin and sold to American GIs serving in Vietnam; some thirty thousand became addicted and brought their habits home, spurring the largest heroin epidemic the United States has ever seen.

Aided by his American advisors, General Vang Pao quickly rose to power in the Royal Lao Army by unifying most of the northeastern Hmong clans in support of the CIA war plan. I have long struggled to understand exactly how he was able to win over so many of his people. In part, he did it by marrying the daughters of several important clan leaders, thereby forging key alliances within the traditional Hmong system of kinship and self governance. But that doesn't explain the villagers' unflagging loyalty to Vang Pao, even after losing so many of their men and boys in the war.

Pro-war historians assert that the Hmong were motivated by an innate cultural opposition to communism, which they feared would destroy their autonomous way of life. The opposing view holds that the key to Vang Pao's influence was American air power. By guaranteeing the sale and transport of the villagers' annual opium harvest, he won the commitment of the village men to train and fight for the CIA. When the male population in the villages declined due to war casualties, there wasn't enough labor left for rice farming, so Vang Pao arranged for USAID helicopters to air drop rice to the hungry villagers. If a village refused to deliver its quota of men and boys to fight in the war, Vang Pao would allegedly withhold the rice. The truth about the charismatic general's power over his people is difficult for an outsider to understand; it may lie somewhere between these extremes.

After the Royal Lao Government fell in May 1975, the CIA evacuated Vang Pao, his seven wives, his top officers, and their immediate families to northern Thailand in the few American aircraft that remained in the region. Meanwhile, tens of thousands of their lower-ranking kinsmen were left behind to fend for themselves against the persecution of the new communist government. On May 9, 1975, the Lao People's Revolutionary Party newspaper declared that "the Hmong must be exterminated to the root."

In hundreds of interviews recorded by UNHCR volunteers, immigration caseworkers, journalists, ethnographers, and others, Hmong refugees recount a living nightmare of burning villages, rape, torture, infanticide, and mass murder at the hands of the Pathet Lao's mostly Vietnamese soldiers. Some describe "yellow rain": chemical weapons sprayed from the air that caused painful respiratory illnesses, skin burns, uncontrollable bleeding and vomiting, birth defects, poisoned crops, and mass deaths. Many Hmong were arrested and taken to forced labor camps, euphemistically called "seminar camps," from which most never returned. Thousands of Hmong villagers who had been willingly or unwillingly drawn into the CIA's war were forced to abandon their homes and go into hiding in the dense hillside jungles that separate their northern homeland from the Mekong River. Always on the move and constantly hunted by the Pathet Lao/Vietnamese soldiers, Hmong families carrying sacks of rice and babies on their backs slowly made their way south through the almost impassable terrain.

Arriving at the banks of the Mekong, many Hmong were shot or drowned while trying to cross the deceptively swift river to reach Thailand. Others crossed at night using makeshift rafts, only to be confronted by hostile Thai soldiers and police on the other side. One refugee likened the situation to "fleeing the tiger to meet the lion." For some Hmong, the concentric rings of ornate silver they had tradition-ally worn around their necks afforded them a means to pay boatmen to ferry them across the river and to bribe the Thai authorities. However, Thai soldiers often robbed them of their silver and other possessions as soon as they disembarked. Those who managed to surmount all of these obstacles spent years living in squalid Thai refugee camps, waiting to be relocated to the United States.

My own understanding of the Secret War is conflicted. I find it dif-ficult, if not impossible, to see any justification for all of the lives that were lost, especially when the operation's chief architect, CIA agent Bill Lair, admits that he knew from the very beginning it was unlikely to succeed. After the United States finally withdrew from Indochina, the so-called dominoes that anti-communist ideologues had long warned about never fell. Thirty-odd years after the war, tourism is booming in the region: vacationing Americans surf Vietnamese beaches and sip "happy shakes" on the banks of the Mekong.

But when I sit in my Hmong friends' living rooms, sharing their ceremonies and meals, a different picture emerges. They are genuinely proud of their service to our country. They believe that they had no alternative but to fight and that their sacrifices were made for a just cause. By all accounts they fought bravely. When American pilots were shot down behind enemy lines, the Hmong went to their rescue. In one case, a Hmong unit lost nearly fifty men rescuing a single American pilot. While

I may have read more books about the war then they have, my Hmong friends actually lived it. They lost fathers, brothers, and sons. They are still haunted by memories of hiding in the jungle, subsisting on a hand-ful of rice a day, always dreading the sound of approaching footsteps and cracking branches. I have but one fragmentary childhood memory of the Secret War, as vivid in my mind as if it had occurred last week: in a flickering black-and-white picture televised from the Oval Office, Richard Nixon leans on his elbows, stares at the camera and, in his low, guttural drawl, pronounces the words "Plain of Jars."

Thirty-five years later my small passenger plane begins its descent and I watch as sawtooth mountains give way to a wide plateau. Chris-tened "Plaine de Jars" by the French, and later shortened to "PDJ" in American military jargon, the Plain of Jars was the principle theater of

conflict in the Secret War. Ringed by dramatic peaks on all sides, the dusty expanse of rolling hills and fields, stitched with streams and dotted with villages, presents a stunning view to the first-time visitor. But as my plane continues to descend, I begin to make out a lunar landscape pockmarked with thousands of bomb craters.

From 1963 to 1972, the United States Air Force, in violation of the Geneva Accords, supported Vang Pao and his Hmong ground troops with an almost ceaseless campaign of bombing strikes. In nine short years, the United States dropped more bombs per capita on Laos than any other country has ever suffered in any other war in history: approximately one ton of bombs for every man, woman, and child living in the country at the time. When cloudy weather obscured the targets, American pilots often emptied their payloads wherever they might fall, in order to conserve fuel for the return flight. Many of the bombs dropped were cluster bombs; upon impact, the outer shell casing exploded and scattered hundreds of baseball-sized "bombies" in every direction. With sufficient impact, each bombie would explode, disintegrating into shrapnel and maximizing collateral damage. Many, however, did not explode. Today millions lie buried in farmers' fields, lodged in stands of bamboo, and scattered throughout the landscape, ready to explode when struck with a farm implement, stepped on, or tossed playfully by an unsuspecting child. Every year, dozens of Hmong and Lao villagers are killed and dozens more are maimed by the rusting thirty-year-old bombies.

From the window of my plane I can see that the bombs did not discriminate; with seeming randomness, they struck hillsides, fields, villages, and even the mysterious groupings of two-thousand-year-old stone jars that now draw increasing numbers of tourists to the region. Ironically, the bomb casings, craters, and ruins of war are also becoming tourist attractions. Nearly every guest house and restaurant in Xieng Khouang has a few rusting mortar shells piled out front to attract business. A tour of the stone jar sites includes a close-up look at several bomb craters and a huge cave that was used by Pathet Lao soldiers as a bomb shelter.

I make a pilgrimage to Xieng Khouang's Old Capital, abandoned after the war due to the prevalence of unexploded ordinance. Here I visit a fourteenth-century Buddhist temple that was bombed in 1970. Only a few of its interior columns remain, along with the charred, disfigured hulk of its giant seated Buddha. The devout still come here to pray, leaving flowers, candles, and incense at its blackened feet.

NEW ARRIVALS

On a sweltering day in 1919 Kaspar Hovannisian stepped off the train at Tulare. Fleeing Armenia after most of his family was massacred by the Ottoman Turks, he followed thousands of fellow refugees to California's Central Valley, whose landscape and climate reminded them of the old country. After Kaspar had worked half a year in the vineyards, a marriage was arranged for him with Siroon Nalbandian. "I came home from high school one day and my father told me I was going to be married a few days later," Siroon later remembered. The couple met for the first time on their wedding day.

Moving into an unpainted wooden house in the middle of a dusty vineyard, the Hovannisians farmed through the Great Depression and raised five sons. Despite pervasive efforts to prevent Armenians from owning land, Kaspar managed to buy right-of-way houses for a dime on the dollar and move them off the highway to unincorporated settlements like Pixley and Tipton. He rented to black sharecroppers and Mexican braceros who, fleeing poverty and oppression in their own homelands, poured into Tulare County looking for work in its orchards, vineyards, and sea of cotton. As the Hovannisian sons came of age, they expanded the family real estate holdings throughout Tulare and Kings counties.

In the 1960s, Kaspar Hovannisian's oldest son, John, began buying up houses and apartment complexes in Fresno. By the time of his father's death, in 1971, John and his brothers had amassed a veritable empire of deteriorating low-income rental property. With his son David as his partner, John established JD Home Rentals, Inc., to manage all of the family's assets. In 1980, just as young David was taking the helm from his father, the U.S. State Department gave him an unexpected gift: thanks to its large inventory of low-income housing, Fresno was chosen as a major destination for the first big resettlement of Hmong refugees. Fueled by successive waves of Hmong and other Southeast Asian immigrants, David Hovannisian

in, leaving a gaping hole in the ceiling. Such complaints went ignored by the Hovannisians for months, even years. Their managers were only authorized to fill vacancies and collect rent, not to make repairs. "Without exception, no one spends John or David Hovannisian's money except John and David Hovannisian," said JD property manager Jerry Saylor in a 1990 court deposition.

In 1988, seven-year-old Melia Vang died four days after falling into a slime-filled JD apartment pool. The algae was so thick that she completely disappeared from view. A teenage boy dived in after her, groping around in the murky water to locate the unconscious girl. The pool had already been cited several times by the Health Department and received three more citations after Melia's death. The Hovannisian's insurance company settled for $150,000 without admitting guilt.

"We cater to Asian tenants because we have very few problems with rent collection or property destruction," JD manager Saylor

expanded his family's slum empire by double digits. By 2001, the family owned an estimated six to eight thousand units, all free and clear.

At the same time, complaints and lawsuits about living conditions at JD properties mounted. Hmong tenants described backed-up sewage; leaking roofs; broken windows and appliances; cockroach, rat, mice, and flea infestations; and a lack of heat, water, and air conditioning. I visited one apartment where the roof had completely caved

continued in his deposition. The Hovannisians developed a foolproof method to boost their occupancy rates: they recruited Hmong managers by offering them half-off rent. The resident managers soon filled the vacancies with their own relatives. One former manager, Xeng Lee, alleged that JD preferred Hmong tenants because many "could not speak English and did not know their rights." A 1997 lawsuit against the company contended that JD used "strong-arm tactics to intimidate and harass tenants, to defraud them into paying rent that is not due or to scare tenants into leaving without due process of law." In 2004 the City of Fresno's Code Enforcement Division spent over a quarter million dollars of its operating budget responding to complaints about JD properties.

David Hovannisian has a collection of classic European cars that he keeps in a secret warehouse in an old industrial part of Fresno that has seen better days. Their chrome insignias bear the names of some of the world's most storied automakers: Mercedes, Ferrari, Jaguar, Alpha Romeo, Rolls Royce. A Hmong man called Tai, born in Laos during the last years of the Secret War, works full-time for Hovannisian; his sole responsibility is the care and maintenance of his boss's prized automobiles, plus a potpourri of antique pinball machines, die-cast model cars, miniature gas engines, and other ephemera from Hovannisian's childhood in the 1950s and 60s. All of these objects are kept in immaculate condition, bubble wrapped, and meticulously organized in the heavily secured warehouse, now packed from floor to ceiling with the accumulated miscellany. Tai is a mechanical and electrical genius who can fix anything that is broken, fabricate any missing part, and restore any kind of machine to its original glory. But his primary mission is looking after Hovannisian's cars. Day after day, he lovingly waxes and buffs them, polishes their gleaming chrome, and rubs mink oil into their leather upholstery. He cleans smudges off white sidewall tires and wipes fingerprints from mirrors. Next, he starts them up, checks their oil, fluids, and tire pressure, tunes them, and makes any necessary repairs. Occasionally he exercises the vehicles with a short drive around the block, carefully wiping the dust off of the tires afterward. It takes him about a month to get through the entire collection. When he finishes the last car he checks his supplies and makes a list of any that need replenishing. Then he begins all over again.

TOUT TOU

Sooner or later every photographer finds his or her muse in a particular place. For Edward Weston, it was the fog-shrouded cliffs of Point Lobos. For Diane Arbus, it was the social melting pot of Central Park. In the spring of 2005, I would find my photographic muse in a cockroach-infested JD apartment complex next to a ditch bank in Central Fresno.

My first look at the place is through the bug-smeared windshield of a social service organization's van. This is a village teeming with life. Hmong families of fifteen and twenty spill out of tired doorways. Vegetable gardens sprout from every available patch of dirt. Kids play soccer on the grimy patio surrounding a kidney-shaped pool now filled in with cement. Old women slit the throats of chickens and pluck their feathers. Laundry dries on the sawed-off stumps of dead trees. Three men squat together in one corner, smoking a mixture of tobacco and opium from a large bong made of black PVC pipe. A young woman with Down Syndrome comes up to the van to greet our driver. Now I sorely regret the decision not to bring my camera on this first visit.

These are the new arrivals. In 2003, the Thai government announced that it would close the Hmong refugee camp at Wat Tham Krabok, the largest one remaining in the country. The U.S. State Department, UNHCR, and various relief organizations scrambled to prepare for resettling one last big wave of Hmong immigrants to the United States, France, and Australia. A delegation from Fresno that included doctors, dentists, psychologists, social workers, and politicians visited the camp, preparing a report on the condition of the refugees for local service agencies who would soon be receiving them as clients. My work as a photographer began just as the San Joaquin Valley resettlement was starting to pick up steam; some of the new refugees had already been here for a few months, while others continued to arrive weekly at the airport. Fresno alone would receive nearly three thousand.

My project combines photography, ethnography, and journalism to document the new arrivals as they attempt to maintain their traditional culture and adapt to life in a strange, new world eight thousand miles from their birthplace. Our team includes an anthropologist, several social workers, community activists, and multilingual interpreters. Hmong elders serve as cultural advisors. The project's outcomes include a large museum exhibition and a digital research archive that will make thousands of photographs, oral history interviews, video clips, and other documents available online. Organized as a partnership between several nonprofit cultural and educational institutions, the project has two broad goals: to provide a resource for scholars and to educate Americans of all ethnic backgrounds about the history and culture of their Hmong American neighbors.

A petite Lao woman with a long name—Chanthanome "Tout Tou" Lounbandith Bounthapanya—drives a big gray passenger van through some of Fresno's poorest neighborhoods, picking up and dropping off Hmong refugees for English classes, employment counseling, and other services. I have asked to ride along in order to get a feel for the lay of the land where I will be working for the next five years. I quickly discover that Tout Tou (pronounced "To Too") is much more than a "transportation coordinator," her euphemistic job title. She has an amazing rapport with the refugees, greeting each one by name as he or she climbs into the van, and asking for the latest news of their families. She keeps up a lively banter with them in Thai, the lingua franca of Southeast Asian refugees. As we drive past rows of faded stucco apartment buildings and rundown tract houses, Tout Tou points out the homes of Hmong families she thinks I might be interested in photographing: "That family over there has thirteen kids. The one across the street just lost their son in a shooting. Tomorrow they are going to do a ceremony and kill a cow."

Tout Tou is a Laotian refugee from the southern province of Savannakhet. Her maternal grandfather, a prosperous businessman, told her mother never to marry a soldier, which she did in spite of the warning. After the war, Tout Tou's family was arrested and sent to a series of forced labor camps in Laos and Vietnam, where they spent ten years. One night, without saying a word to anyone, Tout Tou's father escaped from the camp and disappeared into the jungle. A week later, her mother followed suit, leaving fifteen-year-old Tout Tou and her thirteen-year-old brother despondent. Tout Tou noticed that some of the guards went home at night, while those who stayed often slept on the job. After making their own nocturnal escape, she and her brother embarked on a nightmarish six-month journey, finally reuniting with their parents at Nong Seng refugee camp in Thailand.

My day-long tour of the Fresno Hmong world is nearly complete. We have seen all of the big Central and Southeast apartment complexes, Sin City, South Clovis, and a few Hmong farms near Highway 99 and Jensen. I keep thinking about that apartment complex by the canal; I can't wait to return with my camera. But the biggest discovery of the day is Tout Tou; she will be indispensable to the project. As the gray January day dims to dusk, it starts to drizzle on our windshield. I glance down and notice for the first time that Tout Tou is driving barefoot.

SEEING

The Xiong family has nine children, three of whom are blind. We meet them after their first week in Fresno; they are all huddled together on two couches, sharing blankets and sick with a feverish flu. In addition to his blindness, the oldest teenage boy's face is a mass of scar tissue, resulting from exposure to chemical weapons; some spots are bleeding and bandaged. He is flanked by two sisters; the younger one looks frightened and trembles with fever, the older one is maturing into a beautiful young woman, in spite of her circumstances. A younger blind boy with large blue cataracts is squeezed against the armrest to her left. On the bigger couch, the mother cradles an infant, surrounded by five young children. The smallest blind boy dozes at her feet; his skin shows yellowish signs of jaundice.

Three social workers have come along with Tout Tou and me to assess the needs of this family, which seem overwhelming. The social workers sit stiffly on folding chairs, squarely facing the family on their end-to-end couches. The father, Neng Xiong, sits off to one side in a dining chair; he is the sole family member who is not sick and does most of the talking. Tout Tou and I sit on the floor.

With Tout Tou translating in Thai and English, Neng tells us an amazing story about the abbess of a Buddhist temple who once saved his life. He still wears the cleric's picture in a locket around his neck.

I scoot closer to one of the couches and measure the light through my camera. Despite the dark winter day, a sliding glass door to one side provides beautiful, if weak, portrait lighting on the faces of the children. Using a tripod from my low position on the floor, I make a few test exposures to see how the kids will react to the camera. They are amazingly tolerant of it. I move in closer, shooting pictures of the mother and children on the left-hand sofa. But my real goal is to photograph Jong, the ten-year-old blind boy on the other couch.

Unlike his older blind brother, disfigured by chemical exposure, Jong's face is powerfully expressive. Flame blue cataracts set against his mahogany skin give his eyes an eerie, far-off light, as though he sees things the rest of us cannot. Earlier, as the interview began, I studied the boy's movements carefully. He seemed to react to things that were being said, shifting the angle of his head and the direction of his gaze. He seemed to respond to air currents and the movements of other people in the room. Maybe he could see the *dab*.

In almost every photographic situation there is one overriding image that cries out to be captured. Sometimes it is a picture that perfectly sums up the story or place. Other times it is an anomalous subject that goes against the grain of everything around it. Sometimes it is just a picture you have to have and you don't know why. Most of the time, photographers fail to get this ultimate picture, but there is always the next shoot. From the moment I walked in the room, I knew that, if I came away with no other image, I had to capture the strange light in that boy's eyes.

I pick up my tripod and scoot along the floor to the other sofa, setting up in front of Jong. My vertical frame is too wide so I scoot closer. Still too wide. I keep moving in, refocusing on the sapphire eye nearest the lens. Finally the frame is about right. Now I can sense him sussing me out, using his acute hearing and smell to form a mental image of me.

He cocks his head from one side to the other. I refocus on the moving eye but do not make any exposures. His range of facial expression is amazing. Sometimes his eyes open wide or roll upward as if possessed by a divine light.

I begin to make a few exposures. I feel he can see me perfectly, but not with his eyes. I make more exposures, straining to keep up with his small movements. The depth of field is very shallow, so the slightest change in the angle of the boy's face or movement of his eyes requires a focus adjustment. I click off frame after frame, worrying that my focus might be a bit off or that I haven't quite caught the right moment yet; I never know when to quit. Now there is no more sound and no one else left in the room but Jong and me, and it feels as if we have been here for hours trying to make this picture. There is nothing left but the shifting focus and the moving eye and the silent clicking of the shutter and Jong somehow seeing me better than I see him.

After the interview, and after I have made the requisite pictures for the project archive, we all go out in the backyard for mug shots. Tout Tou loves having her picture taken with every family we visit. The families also enjoy getting the 8x10 prints I make for them. I figured out early on in the project that the Hmong don't really care for the documentary pictures I shoot—they much prefer formal portraits posed in front of flowers or trees—so I always make sure to shoot a few of those pictures to give them.

The Hmong have their own unique style of commercial portrait photography. They love to be photographed in front of large canvas backdrops hand painted with scenes of waterfalls, flower gardens, bamboo forests, lakes, or iconic subjects such as the Great Wall of China. The photographic style in America is almost identical to that seen in Laos, except that the American Hmong often use backdrops with politically charged wartime scenes, like the secret landing strip at Long Cheng,

complete with an improbable number of fighter planes and helicopters filling the skies. One giant, panoramic backdrop at Fresno's Hmong New Year Festival shows hundreds of Hmong with all of their possessions on their backs, mobbing the runway in the hope of crowding aboard an American C-47 that will soon evacuate the luckier among them to Thailand. The tarmac is littered with piles of worthless Lao currency.

Dressed in their finest New Year costumes, Hmong families are photographed smack up against the painted backgrounds of their choice. They stand on green AstroTurf with pots of artificial flowers clustered around their feet. The smiling photographer gently poses his customers, then moves back to his tripod and counts to three—*ib, ob, peb*—click. Afterward the digital images are heavily retouched, removing all of the subjects' skin blemishes and wrinkles, boosting the color, and leaving their faces looking impossibly smooth and painterly. Photography and painting are thus merged into a beautiful folk art form with a vague undercurrent of surrealism.

POLYGAMY

The first time we visit the family of Toua Moua Vang (a pseudonym) there are thirty-four people living in his four-bedroom rental house. The coatrack in the entryway is full—but not with coats. Instead, some twenty-four *qeej* ("keng") hang from the rack or lean in the corners. The Hmong play these curved bamboo instruments at funerals to ward off bad spirits and guide the soul of the deceased back to its birthplace. *Qeej* players stalk the bad spirits like mine sweepers. Crouching low and bending over their rhinoceros-horn-shaped instruments, they prowl around near the body of the deceased in a slow, circular dance. Blowing into long, vertical mouthpieces and fingering holes in the bundled bamboo, they produce low, wheezing tones that have a strangely calming effect on the listener. Every now and then they will suddenly whirl about and scurry off in hot pursuit of errant *dab* (spirits).

Toua Moua Vang is a *qeej* master. Nearly every weekend he is booked to play at least one Hmong funeral. He also builds and sells the instruments, and teaches others how to play them. These skills bring him a good cash income and a lot of respect in the local Hmong community. After only five months in Fresno, the Vang family is relatively prosperous compared to other new arrivals. Most of the young adults in the household already have jobs despite speaking almost no English.

But the most unusual thing about Toua Moua is that he has two wives living together in the same house. Normally the State Department breaks up polygamous Hmong families, consigning each wife and her children to different residences. But somehow this family has managed to fly under the radar, and they all live together under one roof with their many children and grandchildren.

Toua Moua Vang is forty-two. His first wife, Mai Xiong, is forty-eight; she was previously married to one of Toua Moua's uncles. After the uncle died, Toua Moua married Mai out of a cultural obligation to take care of her. Years later, he met his second wife, Ka Vue, who is now thirty-seven. She had been

Fascinated by this family and encouraged by their openness, I return again and again to photograph them. Sometimes I am overwhelmed by their sheer numbers. There always seem to be people everywhere, coming and going from bedrooms and hallways, sitting together in little groups here and there on the living room floor, but never staying in one place for more than a few minutes. Kids play everywhere and the doors are constantly banging at both ends of the house. Hmong videos run nonstop on a flickering television that nobody in particular watches. Somebody is always cooking up a huge pot of rice in the kitchen while others chop vegetables or hack away at freshly butchered meat. Outside, Toua Moua and his uncles carve mouthpieces for their *qeej* in a shed next to the chicken coop. Young boys play an ancient Hmong game with small stones in the middle of the driveway, behind Toua Moua's secondhand SUV.

I follow the Vang family for several months. Ka, the pregnant second wife, gets a little bigger every time I see her. During Hmong New Year, I photograph her getting into her costume with some difficulty in front of a tall plate glass mirror that leans against one wall of the bedroom. She keeps having to let out the skirt and adjust the silver coins to accommodate her expanding girth. One afternoon the following spring, just a couple of weeks before Ka is due to give birth, Tout Tou and I drop by for an impromptu visit after calling first. The day is unseasonably hot and Ka is lying on the couch, wearing only a bra and a loose-fitting skirt. She doesn't seem to mind

married once before and already had seven children of her own. Now she and Toua Moua are expecting their first child together. Meanwhile, Toua Moua also has six children with Mai, including several married sons who, along with their wives and children, all live in the home. Rounding out the household are some of Mai's children and grandchildren from her first marriage, and Toua Moua's elderly mother. It can be very complicated for visitors to sort out who is who in this family and how they are related to each other.

our seeing her that way and talks with us for several minutes before getting up and putting on a blouse. The huge, white orb of her pregnant belly is an amazing sight, like a planet with canals of translucent blue veins and deserts of scar tissue from her previous seven births.

No one else is home except for a couple of younger children and a stepdaughter, who is sleeping in the other room. I have never seen this house so quiet. Ka cuts up a pineapple and serves it to us. There isn't much to photograph, so we just sit and talk. Ka and Tout Tou chatter away in Thai, a second language for both of them. Both women were born in Laos and are about the same age, yet the only language they have in common is the one they both learned in Thai refugee camps. As the conversation continues, Tout Tou becomes more animated. I detect a mischievous gleam in her eye as she glances in my direction. "I just asked her how they make love when there are two wives," Tout Tou whispers. "She says they take turns."

Tout Tou has what Dale Carnegie would have described as a "winning personality." With her gregarious charm, she quickly makes friends and gains their confidence. She is fearless when it comes to asking questions. Thus I am not surprised when Ka opens up and tells us all about her polygamous marriages, past and present. As the conversation continues, Tout Tou gives me periodic updates in English: "I asked her what she does when it's not her turn. She says she just lies there and pretends to be asleep."

That afternoon, we learn that harmony in a polygamous Hmong family is determined by fairness. "If one wife gets to go on a trip with her husband, the other one gets to go next time," Ka explains. "The same goes for the bedroom: each wife has her turn on certain nights, and the schedule must not change for any reason. My first husband had three wives, but he treated all of us very badly. He often cheated with other women and would disappear for weeks at a time, so I left him."

Ka's impromptu discourse continues: "When a Hmong man has

several wives, they usually sleep in different partitions of a bamboo house. Each night he stays with a different wife. If the wife whose turn it is happens to be mad at him, then he has to spend the night by himself and may not sleep with another wife. Hmong men who do not treat their wives equally usually end up with broken families," Ka opines. "Toua Moua is a good husband," she confides. "He is always fair to both of us, and our household is a happy one."

Toua Moua and his two wives have always shown great tenderness and respect for one another in my presence. I have made portraits of the three of them together on several occasions. On one visit I watch the older wife, Mai, helping Toua Moua get ready for a funeral. She winds the long sash around his waist and ties it in front, then helps him on with his vest. She fusses over every detail of his clothing, straightening his collar, and smoothing imaginary wrinkles from his white shirt and black silk harem pants. Finally she helps carry his five or six *qeej* out to the car. "She is a good wife," observes a very pregnant Ka, resting nearby on the couch.

JU CHA

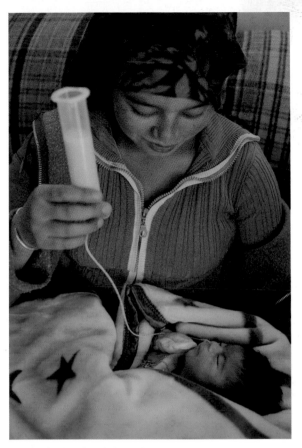

Ju Cha feeding her baby at home.

When Ka Vue's baby finally arrives, Tout Tou and I are invited to the *hu plig*. There is no shaman at this ceremony; the extended family simply gathers to bless the new baby and eat together. But first everyone ties white cotton strings around the mother's and baby's wrists, offering a verbal blessing with each one. Typical blessings include things like living a long life, having lots of children, and making lots of money.

Three folding tables are placed end to end, covered in white cloth, and laden with food. Special ceremonial foods are placed in the center: boiled whole chickens with lit candles protruding from their body cavities; a bowl of eggs, each representing the soul; and a tall, multitiered party tray heaped with fruit, eggs, potato chips, Snickers bars, M&Ms, and dollar bills, all blessings for the mother and her newborn. Relatives are expected to leave larger cash gifts in white envelopes around the party tray.

Meanwhile, on the enclosed back porch of the house, a young mother with a newborn infant about the same age as Ka's baby goes largely ignored by the celebrants. She is Ju Cha, the wife of Toua Moua's oldest son, Chong. Her baby was born prematurely and now, at one month, still weighs less than five pounds. The baby cannot eat normally and must be fed a liquid diet through a slender plastic tube implanted in her nose. Instead of a *hu plig* like the one Ka's baby is having today, a shaman was called to perform a more serious soul-calling ceremony for the baby shortly after she came home from the hospital.

I had photographed Ju Cha many times in the months leading up to the birth of her second child; the nineteen-year-old mother also has a three-year-old son. Ju caught my photographer's eye the first time I met the family. I could not help but make a connection between her story and that of Dorothea Lange's Migrant Mother, immortalized by the late photographer in a Central Valley farm labor camp during the

1930s. Lange's gritty black-and-white portrait of the woman and her two bedraggled children has come to symbolize the Great Depression in the American mind's eye. Ju would become my migrant mother in dozens of photographs as I followed the story of her family's resettlement in Fresno.

Some Hmong look Chinese, others look Laotian, while still others have what I think of as a pure Hmong look. Ju Cha falls in the last category. She has pale skin, freckles, and delicate, almost Eurasian features. Her hair is a quarter-shade lighter than everyone else's in the family. Working with the Hmong for the past five years, I have often observed these seemingly anomalous physical traits. Not infrequently, one child in a family will be born with very light-colored hair that darkens as the child matures. I photographed an older Hmong man at the Millbrook apartments who looked almost Russian or Siberian; he had reddish hair, hazel-green eyes, and a ruddy complexion. One theory of Hmong origin speculates that they migrated to southern China more than four thousand years ago from Central Asia or Siberia.

Three weeks after the *hu plig*, Ju Cha's baby is near death and must be rushed to Children's Hospital. A feeding tube is inserted in her stomach and she must remain in the intensive care unit for an indefinite time. Ju never leaves her side. Tout Tou calls me with the news and encourages me to go visit them. Unfortunately, she cannot accompany me; her superior job performance has earned her a promotion and she now works in the office as an employment counselor. I have just lost my best translator.

The drive to Children's Hospital of Central California is a surreal experience. Perched on the desolate bluffs of the San Joaquin River, the giant pastel-colored structure looms on the horizon like an unfinished movie set. In a backroom deal with a developer who donated the land, the hospital's board voted to vacate its original facility in Central Fresno and rebuild on this isolated site a county away. Here the developer hopes to sprawl a new city of red tile roofs and strip malls in spite of the fact that there is no water. However, he didn't count on the fact that it is harder for an outsider to buy Madera County supervisors' votes than it is for a well-connected local, so the shiny new facility now languishes on the parched bluffs like a beached whale. Meanwhile, the hospital's mostly indigent patients, many of whom depend on public transportation, must now find a way to make the ten-mile journey north, crossing the river via a congested two-lane bridge.

I follow a long hallway to the intensive care unit, where I am escorted to a small room. Ju Cha stands wearily over her baby. Tubes and wires seem to emanate from every part of the sleeping infant's body. Assorted monitoring devices beep, flash, and hum in arythmic synchronicity. Toua Moua's older wife, Mai, has organized a highly efficient support system to deliver freshly cooked food, changes of clothes, and anything else Ju needs around the clock. Ju's husband comes every evening after work, but her three-year-old boy is not allowed in the ICU due to the risk of infection. Ju occasionally sleeps for an hour or so on a recliner chair next to the baby's gurney.

The image of nineteen-year-old Ju standing over her baby surrounded by all of the postmodern wires, tubes, bandages, and electronic monitoring devices is a photograph begging to be made. She is a twenty-first-century Madonna. Even the angle at which she holds her head while gazing at the baby and the way that her hair frames her delicate face evokes Titian, Raphael, Da Vinci. More importantly, this single image captures the essence of Ju's story: her incredible devotion to motherhood and her long journey between two worlds separated by eight thousand miles and two hundred years. Even the lighting is perfect: subdued overhead spots throw a halo of soft, ethereal light over Ju and the baby, leaving the background in near darkness.

After using up most of my Hmong vocabulary with greetings and pleasantries, I search the hallways until I find a Hmong nurse who can translate for me. I ask the nurse to ask Ju if I can take the photograph. With a very respectful Lao-style *nop* (hands pressed together as in prayer, accompanied by a slight bow), Ju thanks me for offering but says she prefers that I wait until the baby is better. Over the past four months we have made countless photographs together and this is the first time she has ever turned me down. I ask the nurse to tell Ju that this picture is very important; it will show everyone what a devoted mother she is, and it will also tell the story of her people and their long journey to America. However, Ju remains polite but firm in her resolve not to do the photograph today. If only Tout Tou were here.

The nurse goes back to work and I sit with Ju and the baby in silence. Mentally, I calculate the aperture, shutter speed, and focal distance I will need to make the photograph. Without lifting the camera to my eye, I study the scene and note precisely where the corners of the frame will go. If I am careful, one quick exposure is all I will need. Only a single click of the shutter to atone for. Maybe she won't even hear it amongst all of the whirring, humming, and beeping machinery, I rationalize.

I flash back to the time a Hmong family invited me to photograph the funeral of their revered clan leader, Neng Thao Lee. News of his death came as a shock to everyone in the family; he had appeared to be in perfect health. I was invited to take photographs and given a badge to wear that said "family member." But there was one unusual stipulation: I was not to photograph the body under any circumstances. In the dozen or so Hmong funerals I had previously photographed, I had never faced this prohibition.

The funeral was a large one; relatives came from all over the country and General Vang Pao made an appearance with his usual entourage of six body guards dressed like Secret Service men in suits and dark glasses.

The moment arrived when all of the family members gathered around the body and began to weep. The hall was suddenly filled with a loud cacophony of intense wailing, moaning, and sobbing. This happens at every Hmong funeral and can last up to forty-five minutes. No one signals this event; everyone just seems to know when it is time.

Just before the weeping started, I had positioned myself close to the body, so that I could photograph the shaman seated nearby. He chanted continuously into a wireless microphone, performing the traditional Hmong funeral ceremony at a small table. A candle and a short stick of bamboo were his primary accoutrements, but two shot glasses of Bud Light had also been placed on the table as offerings for the soul of the departed. Occasionally the shaman downed the shots himself and refilled the glasses from a pop-top can. While photographing the shaman, I would occasionally swing my wide-angle lens sharply to the left and grab a quick shot of the mourners surrounding their fallen clan leader; he was laid out in a gorgeous black and purple embroidered robe, befitting his status. "Hlaw Neng," as he was respectfully called by everyone in the family, had played a vital role in his community. He had mediated disputes and served as counselor, psychologist, and father figure to several hundred members of his extended family. In an op-ed piece for the Fresno *Bee*, our project anthropologist, Hank Delcore, described the late clan leader's importance:

> At all hours of day and night, Hlaw Neng responded to calls from clanmates who faced some of life's most intractable problems: parents who had lost control of their children, married couples on the verge of divorce, accusations of domestic abuse. In one case, he was called to a home where a man was pointing a gun at his own head. While other members of his clan and community slept, Hlaw Neng was often up at the wee hours of the morning, because some situations do not wait for daylight. He was known as a man who was unfailingly rational and calm. When others acted rashly, he responded with reason, fairness and the wisdom that comes with age and experience.

The passing of Hlaw Neng was too important an event to be left out of the historical archive in which these photographs would eventually reside. Without the image of the clan leader himself, surrounded by his many mourners, the story of his contribution to the community would never be complete for future generations of Hmong who will visit the online archive to learn about their history. Weighing these considerations against the admonition not to photograph the body, I decided that taking the photograph was the right thing to do. Two weeks later I mailed a CD of the images to Pang Lee, Hlaw Neng's eldest daughter, in North Carolina. I was surprised when her handwritten note card arrived at my office in less than a week's time:

> My family and I thank you for your beautiful pictures. I have not taken a photo with my father since I was a young girl. So the photo of me standing close to him is priceless. Don't ever take your father for granted like I did. One day he will be gone and you will regret everything you did not do for him. Now at least I have this photo to remember him.

My gamble had paid off. I made another CD of the pictures for the Fresno clan members and they were very happy to receive them. No one even seemed to remember that I had been told not to photograph the body.

But today at the hospital is different. The camera is ready, the light is perfect, but I do not take the picture. The camera feels heavy around my neck. I feel the weight of the room, of the entire building. I look at Ju, the perfect Madonna. She is my Migrant Mother, the Hmong equivalent of the one Dorothea Lange photographed some seventy years ago, less than an hour's drive from the hospital. Here is the defining image of the last Hmong resettlement, yet I am incapable of recording it.

Ju smiles at me—the same smile I remember seeing one day when I happened to run into her coming out of an ESL class clutching the first

Pang Lee (left) grieves the loss of her father, Hlaw Neng Thao Lee, Fresno, 2007.

photographs I ever gave her. She speaks softly to me in Hmong, going on at some length. I listen hard but cannot understand more than an occasional word. I think she might be trying to tell me why she doesn't want to do the photograph. Perhaps she is afraid it might disturb the *dab* and somehow jeopardize the baby's chances of recovery. Not knowing enough Hmong to reply, I just smile awkwardly at her. She smiles at me again with that same radiant smile and looks at me for a long time. I stay a little while longer, then get up to leave. *"Sib ntsib dua"* ("See you again"), she says as I walk out the door. After two more months of confinement in this small room, Ju Cha and her baby girl will finally go home.

IMPROVISATION

As we pull up to the stoplight, a Hmong man runs out into the middle of the intersection holding a live chicken at arm's length and waving it around. His son had an accident here the day before and he is trying to recover the lost soul from the *dab* that are lurking nearby. The Hmong believe that the bad *dab* often reside in a particular place, lakes being the most common. About ten years ago, a Hmong teenager from Fresno visited Huntington Lake on a high school field trip and glimpsed a huge dragon swimming beneath the surface of the water. When she saw its yellow eye gazing up at her from the depths, she became so frightened that she blacked out. The fear would not leave her for months. When she lay down at night and closed her eyes she would see the monster staring at her and could not sleep. She was afraid to go anywhere alone, afraid to enter a dark room, afraid to go near water of any kind, even refusing to bathe. After six months, her family called a shaman, who performed two *ua neeb* ceremonies to rescue the girl's soul from the lake-dwelling *dab*. The first, which involved sacrificing a pig, failed to allay her fear. The second, in which a goat was killed, finally did the trick.

Today I am trying out a new photographic strategy with a new translator, Kristie Lee, an off-duty social worker. We have no appointment to interview anyone, no preconceived plan, no schedule, and we are not accompanied by any other social workers. We are simply driving through Hmong neighborhoods in Central Fresno, open to whatever opportunities for photography might present themselves. As I wait for the traffic light to change, Kristie jumps out to talk with the man waving the chicken around. By the time I cross the intersection and pull over, it is too late for photographs, but Kristie already has the story.

We decide to drop by the Millbrook apartments. Many months have passed since I first saw them. The

Another regular fixture is a mentally disabled man of indeterminate age with heavy, black eyebrows; he slinks around the complex, as if harboring some dark secret. Wearing black high-top tennis shoes, he drags one leg behind him in a strange shuffling gait, glancing about suspiciously and muttering to himself. At home he eats every meal alone, squatting in the corner of his family's tiny apartment kitchen. The gardens have grown taller since I was last here, and the new arrivals have settled in. But the feeling of this place being yet another refugee camp has not changed.

A pregnant seventeen-year-old sweeps the porch in front of an open doorway; her three-year-old boy clings to her skirt. Kristie asks to speak with the head of the household and the girl summons her middle-aged father-in-law. Barely two sentences are exchanged before he invites us in. Over and over I will witness this amazing performance as Kristie opens the doors to one Hmong household after another

Indian summer evening brings people outdoors as the afternoon heat begins to dissipate. Slanting sunlight illuminates the open courtyards, enlivening every dilapidated surface it touches. Parents and grandparents sit around the patio in folding chairs, visiting with their neighbors. Kids play everywhere they can run, jump, or climb. Blia Vang, the amiable young woman with Down Syndrome, greets us and follows us around, as she will every time we return. She seems to be the self-appointed ambassador for the complex and takes her responsibilities seriously.

with only the briefest of introductions. She seems to have been born without the nearly universal Hmong trait of shyness, approaching complete strangers without the slightest hesitation and asking if we can come in to their houses and take photographs. Once inside, she makes herself right at home, chatting affably with family members and helping me collect valuable information for the project archive.

Kristie was born in Xieng Khouang Province, near the Plain of Jars, just weeks before General Vang Pao left the country. During the first five years of her life, her family lived on the run with twenty-three related families, mostly hiding in the jungle. The entire group was eventually captured by Vietnamese soldiers and placed in the temporary custody of a pro-communist Hmong village; the captives knew they would eventually be taken away to seminar camps. After a small band of Hmong guerillas staged a daring rescue and freed the families, they scattered and made their way south to the Mekong River. During this last leg of the journey, Kristie's father, who today is even smaller than she is, carried her on his back atop a large sack of rice.

Right away I notice that working in Hmong translation is much more fluid than using Thai, the language of the camps. Kristie is lightning fast, switching languages effortlessly without missing a beat. Now that she is my primary translator I notice that the kinds of images I make are changing. Without the team of social workers conducting prearranged interviews, our shoots are much more spontaneous and productive. By just showing up at an apartment complex and walking into randomly chosen households, we come much closer to capturing Hmong refugee life as it happens.

The inside of the apartment is dim and smoky. The tiniest Hmong woman I have ever seen is cooking in the narrow 1960s-era kitchen; its low counters nearly reach the height of her shoulders. Her middle-aged face seems incongruous atop her childlike body. In the living room, the bare, white monotony of the walls is interrupted only by a modest shamanic altar on one side of the room and a Thai calendar on the other. Members of the four-generation household come and go frequently, pausing to sit briefly on mismatched pieces of thrift store furniture or short Asian stools. Kristie and I have our work cut out for us trying to sort out who is who in this family.

The oldest family member, Va Ser Chang, does not move from the Western-style chair on which he is perched with one knee up to his chest

Va Ser Chang, a new arrival at age ninety-nine.

and the other leg dangling below. His son tells us that he is ninety-nine years old and left the camp in Thailand only a few weeks ago. He may be one of the oldest refugees ever to make the long journey. Clad in the traditional Black Hmong tribal costume of widely flared pantaloons cinched up to his bare chest and a high-collared jacket worn unbuttoned, the old man presents an image at once regal and tattered. His storied flesh stretches thinly over a gaunt frame, revealing the underlying bone structure in stark detail; through the opening in his jacket you can count every rib. Only a few sparse tufts of gray hair crown the high, furrowed dome of his forehead. Yet his eyes sparkle with life and his measured movements exude a slow-motion vitality.

As I start to photograph the old man, he brightens noticeably and appears to bask in the attention of the camera, subtly altering his body position after each exposure. Taking advantage of the ample white walls and ceiling, I bounce my flash off of them at different angles to achieve soft portrait lighting. The old man is amazingly photogenic; each slight change of pose inspires me to make more exposures. My exposures, in turn, inspire him to come up with new poses. Suddenly my throat is burning and tears well up in my eyes. Everyone in the room starts coughing and rubbing their eyes. The small woman in the kitchen has burned a skillet full of hot peppers, filling the entire apartment with stinging smoke. Calmly, as if this were an everyday occurrence, the old man gets out of his chair and slowly makes his way toward the sliding glass door at the back of the apartment. I follow him out to the tiny cubicle garden, where he squats on the door stoop and clears his lungs. Except for the high wooden fence painted cost-saving battleship gray, I feel like I could be in Laos. Tall rows of corn compete with a multitude of bushy Asian vegetables, herbs, and peppers for the scant square footage of available soil. I photograph the old man as he squats on the stoop, gazing into the dying light of dusk. He seems to be contemplating the larger things now, having relinquished all but the barest necessities of his material existence. Looking at him, I see my own mortality. We sit together in silence as dusk turns to dark.

After the worst of the smoke has cleared, I follow the old man back into the apartment, where all of the doors and windows have been thrown open to let in the night air. I still can't get over the sight of him walking barefoot in his black tribal costume; even in Laos, such traditional wear is becoming increasingly rare as Chinese traders on motorbikes bring cheap, Walmart-style clothing to all but the most remote mountain villages. As I pack my camera gear, Kristie and I begin to say our thank yous and goodbyes. Then I notice that the old man has arranged himself into yet another irresistible pose and I am obliged to unpack the camera for a few more exposures. Even Kristie comments on his ability to strike one amazingly expressive pose after another. Just before we leave, it occurs to me to ask the old man what he thinks of life in America so far. His face lights up as Kristie translates the reply: "I wish I'd come sooner."

A few doors down, recent arrivals Tee Moua Thao and his family are having a markedly different experience: "Life is hard here because everything is so far away. You can't go anywhere without a car, so you must depend on relatives to come and pick you up. We can't speak the language so we always need someone to translate; if you can't find anyone, you can really get into a lot of trouble. And these bills! So much money to pay every month! Rent, electricity, and other things I don't even understand. In the camps there were no bills; we grew our own vegetables and raised a few animals. The Thai vendors would come around and sell us rice and jugs of drinking water and that was all we needed money for. Of course they overcharged us, but it was nothing compared to the prices here. You can't even bargain at these markets."

Tee Moua, his wife, La Cha, and their three young boys live in a small, barren apartment with few furnishings or possessions. The sliding glass door provides the only outside view: three feet of concrete patio and the high, gray perimeter fence. The boys have nothing to do and no toys to play with, so they run wild, misbehaving and acting out. Their mother is listless and withdrawn, sitting in a fetal position on the couch, surrounded by the empty white walls of her new world. She rarely speaks during our visit. Tee Moua himself seems depressed, not knowing what to do next. Outside I photograph one of the boys squatting and playing with a handful of dirt, for lack of anything else.

On another visit, Kristie and I walk through the complex passing out prints to the people we have photographed. The task goes slowly because many of them invite us in and serve us drinks or snacks. In one household we find the young wife of the family home alone and eager to talk. I note an urgency in her voice as the staccato rhythm of the Hmong conversation picks up pace. "I married my husband a few months before we left the camp. My parents, brothers, and sisters all went to North Carolina at the same time we came to Fresno. Now my husband and his family treat me very badly; they make me do all of the hardest work and say cruel things to me all the time. My mother-in-law calls me "bitch" instead of my name. They tell me I am ugly, stupid, and slow; they are always ordering me to hurry up and work faster. At meals, I serve the men first, then the older women. After everyone else has finished I eat by myself. I miss my family so much but I have no way to contact them."

On our previous visit to this household, the husband had claimed

The family of La Cha Thao faces an uncertain future.

to be a shaman and had done most of the talking. Picking up a spirit rattle and pair of split buffalo horns, he demanded to have his picture taken next to the family's small altar, mounted atop an air conditioning unit. But now the young woman informs us that she is the actual shaman in the family. Kristie first suggests a family counseling resource, but the woman says she is afraid to call. So Kristie directs a male Hmong colleague to visit the family on the pretext of doing an evaluation but ultimately to try and mediate the situation and help the woman get in contact with her family in North Carolina.

Tout Tou and I once had a similar experience with another family. Anthropology classifies the Hmong as a patrifocal residence culture, meaning that newlywed brides always leave their families and go to live with their husbands' families. By contrast, the Lowland Lao are classified as a matrifocal residence culture; Lao men usually go to live with their wives' families and Lao women end up being the primary property owners. The occasional situation in which a Hmong bride is treated like an indentured servant by her husband's family is a sad by-product of the Hmong system of arranged, exogamous marriage and patrifocal residence. While the practice is declining rapidly in the United States, it still occurs with some frequency in Laos.

My photographic excursions with Kristie are not always so bleak. On our first visit to a Hmong apartment complex in Clovis, we are treated to a delicious barbecue. The complex consists of a single long row of two-story apartments; in the late afternoon its balconies and lower porches teem with life and its stairs are heavily trafficked with the comings and goings of relatives on their way to and from one another's households. Smoke from several barbecues fills the grassy courtyard. Kristie and I sit on the balcony and enjoy a meal of perfectly marinated barbecue pork, grilled corn, and sticky rice. A woman comes up the stairs to see the shaman next door to us, complaining of a migraine. I put my plate down to go photograph the shaman's simple remedy: a head, neck, and shoulder massage.

After dinner we meet a small, impish man in his seventies, bundled up in black Chinese-style clothing and sporting a black skullcap on his bald pate. He is the busybody of the complex, a constant visitor in everyone else's apartments. Kristie's confusing attempts to communicate with him and his lack of verbal response are soon explained when his English-speaking granddaughter informs us that he is completely deaf. Seeing that I am a photographer, the old man immediately motions for

Deaf musician Wa Yee Vang plays a homemade *nkauj nog ncas*.

me to follow him to his apartment. Grabbing my gear, I can hardly keep pace with him; I soon learn that a quick jog is his normal gait.

The walls of his apartment are almost completely covered with photographs clipped from magazines, calendars, and advertising posters. Rice is stockpiled in a pair of blue fifty-gallon barrels to keep vermin out. My new friend disappears into a bedroom and, one by one, brings out his most prized possessions to show me. The first is a framed photograph of him and his late wife, which I estimate to have been taken about twenty-five years ago; they are dressed in Chinese Hmong New Year costumes and stand proudly in front of a painted cherry blossom backdrop. Next he brings out a *nkauj nog ncas* (a traditional string instrument) that he has made from a lychee fruit can, a slender piece of wood, and several strings. He demonstrates how it is played with a primitive bow, deafness apparently not affecting his abilities as a musician. Next comes a kind of tambourine and then a carved wooden flute. The latter is played sideways and produces an eerily beautiful sound; I am not certain if it is the sound he would intend it to be if he could hear, but it is haunting nevertheless.

The most curious thing about the flute is a fluorescent orange prescription medicine bottle that has been affixed to one end. For the Hmong, music is traditionally played for healing and spiritual purposes, not for entertainment. Whatever was in that now-empty prescription bottle must have worked so well that the deaf musician ingeniously decided to combine the best of Hmong and Western medicine. Here is a small, brilliant example of the Hmong American cultural fusion that I am constantly seeking to capture; this time it will require a close-up lens.

HMONG AMERICANS

After months of focusing exclusively on new-arrival families, I begin to see how different they are from the established Hmong families who were part of the earlier waves of immigration. Many of the new arrivals lived more than twenty years in Thai refugee camps, where they had no legal status, could not venture outside of the perimeter fence, and depended on international aid workers and opportunistic Thai vendors to supply most of their material needs. Many of the younger refugees were born in these camps and have come to America with no memory of village life in Laos or the total disruption of it that the war brought. As such, their cultural practices have naturally changed in response to the new surroundings. For example, the popular "story cloth" form of narrative embroidery was actually created in the refugee camps as a way to earn income by selling the quilt-like wall hangings to aid workers; in Laos, only the ancient *paj ntaub* ("pan dao") form of embroidery using abstract design motifs was practiced. By contrast, the story cloth tableaus employ a flat, map-like perspective to depict violent scenes of the war at the top of the frame, Hmong families crossing the river in the middle of the frame, and scenes from Thai camp life at the bottom of the frame, where large passenger planes wait to carry the refugees to America.

During the first year of our documentary project, funding from the California Council for the Humanities mandated that we focus exclusively on new-arrival Hmong families and the housing challenges they faced. The following year, with additional funding from the James Irvine Foundation, we were able to broaden our focus and include families from the earlier waves of immigration, as well as covering village life in northern Laos. We found that, in many ways, the early-arrival families practice a purer form of Hmong culture than do the new arrivals because the former have spent more of their lives in Laos and less time in the Thai camps.

stayed at the Lee house in Fresno for four months, receiving daily care until he recovered. Whenever Yer goes to visit her relatives in St. Paul, word gets out quickly and she is soon inundated with so many requests for her services that she ends up spending most of her vacation performing ceremonies, an exhausting regimen that the sixty-one-year-old shaman cheerfully accepts as part of her calling. When not traveling, she performs ceremonies in local Hmong homes nearly every weekend.

On a visit to the Lee home in 2005, I relax in the living room with several family members, including Yer's relatives who are visiting from Laos. We all share a good laugh about one of Wa's deceased cousins who had seven wives. "They were our aunts, but we could never remember what to call them," David recounts.

Suddenly, Yer changes the subject and makes a short, impassioned speech to me, with one of the kids translating: "I love you just like one of my own sons. From now on I will always think of you as my son, and I hope you will come to visit me more often." With that simple declaration, I become the tallest member of the Lee clan. Whenever I greet Yer and Wa, I am confronted anew by the dramatic differences in our height—mine six-four and theirs well under five feet. I have to bend way over to hug Yer, then remain in a somewhat stooped position to shake hands with Wa, who is even shorter than his wife. Underlying the joy of our spontaneous affection is a visceral lesson in physical anthropology: the profound differences in the lives that both we and our ancestors have lived are so starkly apparent in the contrasting physiognomy of our bodies that I never fail to be awed by the miracle of the Lees' survival, our bond of friendship, and the sheer diversity of human experience.

Yer promises to search the spirit realm for a Hmong name to call me. A few weeks later, she finds one: *Pob Tsuas* ("Paw-Choua"), a double entendre reference to my height and to the steep limestone karst formations found throughout the mountains of northern Laos. The name fits perfectly and will serve me well when I travel there.

To learn more about Yer Lee and how she became a shaman during the harrowing years that her family spent hiding in the jungles of Laos, see "Yer Lor Lee: A Hmong Shaman Tells Her Story," on pages 239–249.

LAOS

Hmong Village Life in Laos

Plate 105

Plate 106

Plate 107

Plate 108

Plate 109

Plate 110

Plate 111

Plate 112

Plate 113

Plate 114

Plate 115

Plate 116

Plate 117

Plate 118

Plate 119

Plate 120

Plate 121

Plate 122

Plate 123

Plate 124

Plate 125

Plate 126

Plate 127

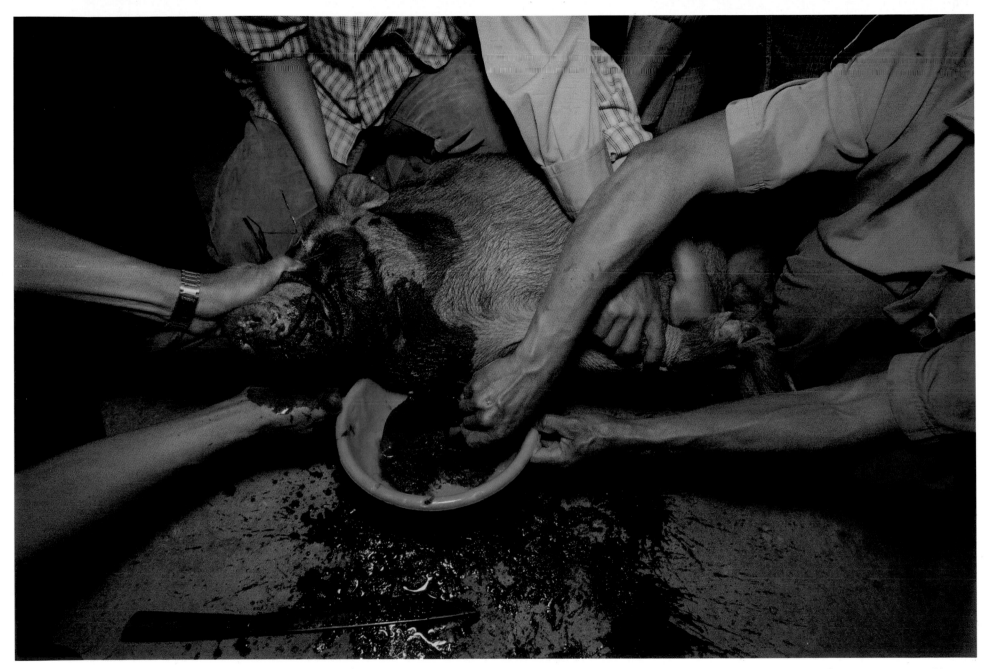

Plate 128

Plate 129

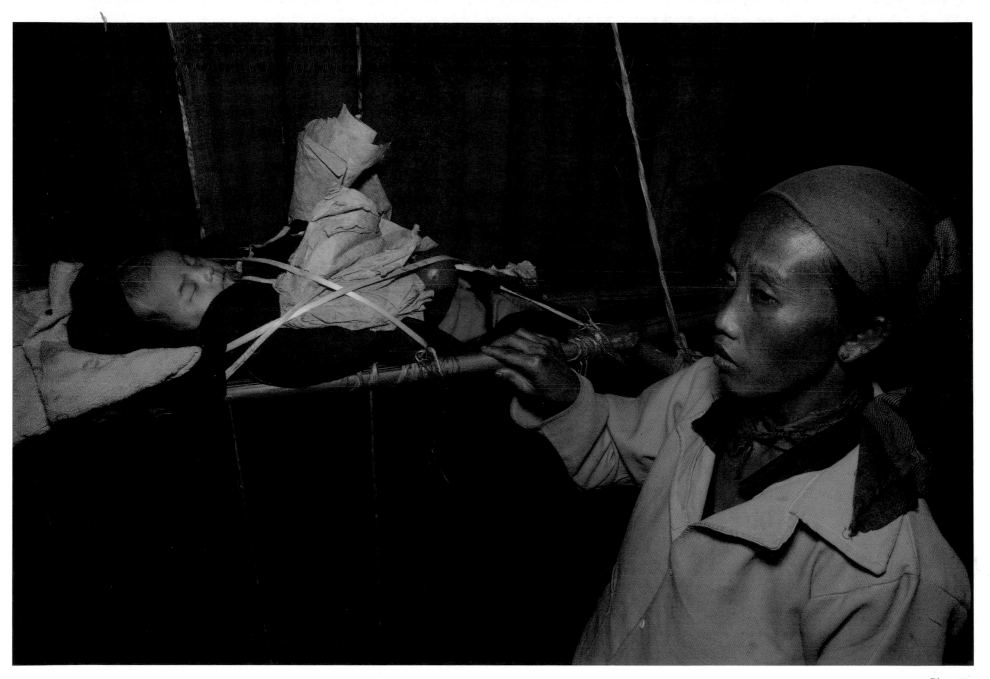

Plate 130

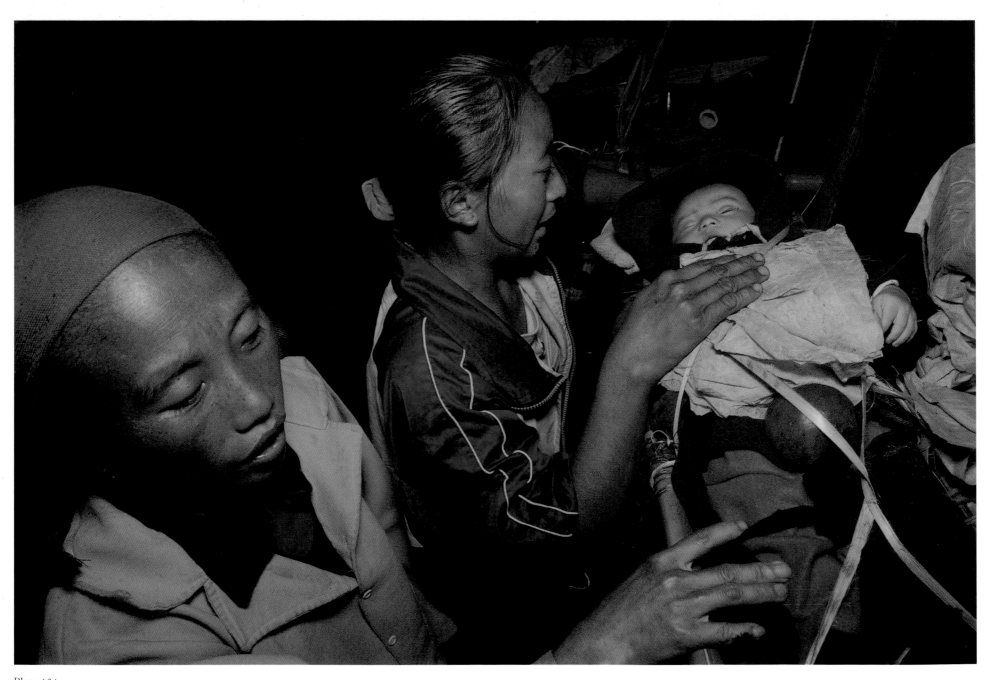

Plate 131

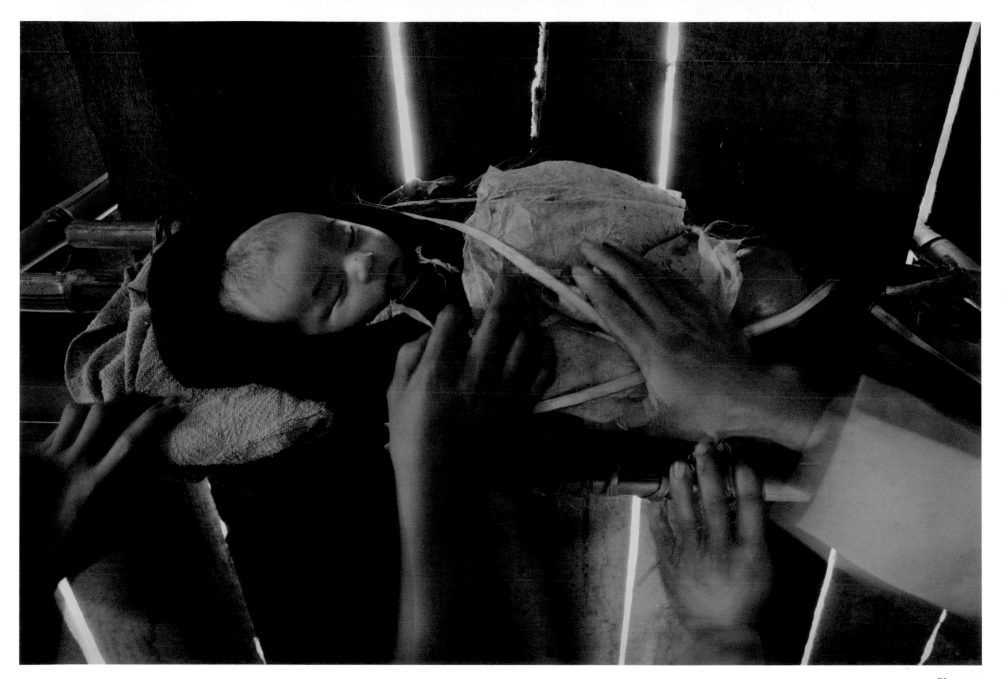

Plate 132

Plate 133

Plate 134

Plate 135

Plate 136

Plate 137

Plate 138

Plate 139

Plate 140

Plate 141

Plate 142

Plate 143

Plate 144

Plate 145

Plate 146

Plate 147

Plate 148

Plate 149

Plate 150

Plate 151

Plate 152

Plate 153

Plate 154

Plate 155

Plate 156

Plate 157

Plate 158

Plate 159

Plate 160

Plate 161

Plate 162

HARVEST

I climb into the front seat of a weather-beaten minivan as my Laotian driver talks on his cell phone. By now I have gotten used to the fact that the seat belts never work in the vehicles I rent here; without fail either the buckle will be broken or one half of the belt will be missing entirely. This time, the metal tongue on the right has been hacked off; most likely it was needed for an improvised motor repair somewhere in the mountainous countryside of Xieng Khouang Province.

We drive to the end of the provincial capital's modest main street and turn east on Route Seven, a bumpy two-lane road that winds lazily out of town and continues all the way to Hanoi. During the war, Route Seven was the sole conduit that carried Vietnamese troops and supplies to Lao communist strongholds in the Plain of Jars. Consequently, fighting was very heavy along the road and today it is lined with bomb craters. Villagers have found many ingenious uses for the craters, turning some into ponds for raising fish or ducks, and filling others with fertile topsoil for vegetable gardens.

A few miles out of town, rolling hills give way to a wide river valley flanked by dramatic mountains on either side. Lao, Khmu, and Hmong villages are scattered along the road, each recognizable by its distinctive architecture and the look of its people. We pass a small group of Khmu women bathing next to a roadside crater-pond. Wrapped in sarongs, they drench themselves with buckets of pond water, their long dark hair and brown skin glistening in the morning sun. Farther along the road, thick-horned water buffalo graze in quilted rice paddies, chewing on the stubble left after the harvest. In the distance, five Buddhist monks walk single file through a golden field on their way back to a primitive country temple. A shaft of sunlight sets their orange robes ablaze against the blue wall of mountain rising behind them. Despite the devastation of two recent wars, Laos remains a profoundly beautiful country.

We drive along in silence for the first hour, taking it all in. My Hmong guide, Long Vang, rides in the back seat, studying a map. Long is a postwar child of the Plain of Jars, struggling to put his village upbringing behind him through education. Graduating from the local community college at the top of his class, only a lack of funding prevented him from attending a four-year university. He is literate and highly proficient in Hmong, Lao, and English. His Hmong literacy is especially noteworthy in a country where it is officially discouraged. Written Hmong only came into being in 1952, when a French missionary, Father Yves Bertrais, devised an early prototype of the RPA writing system now widely used throughout the Diaspora. Long learned to read and write the language from his grandfather, a low-level commander in the war. He is unabashedly pro–Vang Pao and pro-American; his great dream is to live in the United States. Every year he asks me if I know any Hmong girls in California who would like to marry him.

Today our goal is to reach Ban Pha Keo, a Hmong village high in the mountains where I hope to photograph the rice harvest. Elsewhere in the province, the harvest is mostly finished, but the farmers of Ban Pha Keo are still at it, delayed by the cooler microclimate of their high-altitude fields. Underlying my interest in the rice harvest is a deeper desire to seek out Hmong culture in its most traditional form, as little touched by the twenty-first century as possible. By traveling to the most remote, isolated villages in Laos, I hope to see or learn something that will enlighten my understanding of a people who remain mysterious to me despite the years I have spent studying them.

Ban Pha Keo certainly meets my criteria; it was founded in 1975 by a group of Hmong families from Long Cheng who made the grueling journey to their new home on foot. While most refugees fled southwest toward the Mekong River, this group went the opposite direction, heading for the highest inhabitable mountains they could find. Today I will learn the hard way why the Vietnamese soldiers never bothered to go after them.

After another hour of driving we turn onto a bumpy dirt road and follow it past a large Hmong village. We stop briefly to pick up two friends who will accompany us on the hike to Ban Pha Keo; both are unemployed guides who have decided to come along out of curiosity about a place they have heard about all of their lives but never seen. A mile farther down the dirt road, the driver drops us off at the trailhead, which seems little more than a cattle path. We follow it for fifty yards to the biggest bomb crater I have ever seen; it is at least forty feet in diameter and very deep, judging by the dark green water that fills it. A Hmong villager cuts a very small figure as he fishes from its elevated rim.

From there we begin a long descent, passing a small Khmu village. We continue downhill for several more miles and cross a stream. Cradling my sweaty hiking boots under one arm, I linger midstream, letting my feet luxuriate in its deliciously cool water. Meanwhile, my companions wait impatiently for me, having already splashed across in their flip-flops.

Soon our descent grows steeper and I begin to worry. I know from the map that our destination is a thousand feet higher than our starting point; eventually we will have to regain all of the altitude we are losing so fast. The trail winds precariously around the face of a sheer, cylindrical cliff with an alluring cave high above. Then it begins a series of steep downward switchbacks.

An hour later we are still heading downhill, although the trail is beginning to level off. Abruptly, we arrive at the rim of a deep river gorge. The only option for crossing is a rickety bamboo suspension bridge whose rusting cables are strung between trees on opposite banks of the river. We decide to cross one at a time; being the heaviest person, I go first. The bridge is overgrown with vines and many of its bamboo sections are missing. Those that remain are untrustworthy. Gripping the skinny cables firmly with both hands, I cautiously test each foothold before placing any weight on it. The entire structure groans and sways

persistent gnats, who are impervious to mosquito repellent. From time to time, we pass Hmong villagers coming downhill from Ban Pha Keo, each balancing a fifty-pound sack of rice on one shoulder. They will sell their meager surplus for a few dollars at one of the villages along Route Seven. This punishing trail is their only connection to the outside world; all goods and supplies must be carried in and out on foot.

After climbing up a steep ridge, we finally reach the rocky summit of the mountain. A broad alpine vista opens up. In the dry season, distances between peaks and ridges are defined by modulating shades of blue haze created by the wood fires that most people in Laos still use for cooking. Foliage is sparser than in the rainy season and colors are muted. From now on, the trail courses over stony terrain in manageable ups and downs, allowing us to take in a wide panorama of the Annamite Range that divides Laos from Vietnam. Apart from the trail, there is no mark of human presence as far as the eye can see.

as I move slowly along, my body bent over to compensate for the low height of the cables. This bridge was not built for *falang* (Westerners).

On the other side we begin our ascent of a nearly vertical wall of jungle. The mountainside faces south and never gets any sun at this time of year, leaving the red earth trail damp and slippery as it zigzags up the steep slope. Carrying forty-five pounds of photography gear on my back, I sweat profusely yet feel chilly in the moist jungle shade. It is impossible to find the right combination of clothing. For two and a half hours we trudge up the endless switchbacks, harassed by swarms of

We stop to rest by a fallen tree and enjoy a snack of small, seedy oranges and sticky rice. I am thankful for my steel-toed hiking boots, which have bounced off more than a few jagged rocks along the trail today. Meanwhile, my companions hike in flip-flops; even though I have yet to see any Laotian use any other kind of footwear in the mountains or jungles, it still astonishes me that they can trek all day with such scant protection. As we sit procrastinating the remaining mile of trail

that separates us from our goal, the conversation turns to the war. I am impressed with my companions' knowledge of a chapter in history that is not taught in Lao schools or available in Lao libraries.

"How do you guys learn all this stuff?" I ask.

"We have poems in Hmong language that tell our story," Long explains. "We memorize them and pass them along from one generation to the next." These twentysomethings know considerably more about their history than do most of their American-born cousins.

After climbing one last steep hill, we are treated to a spectacular view of the village from above. Nestled in a saddle between three rocky peaks, Ban Pha Keo is home to twenty-three Hmong families. The houses are built of weather-darkened wood with packed-earth floors and hand-hewn shake roofs. Pigs, chickens, and small children meander

about in the central dirt area that seems to be ubiquitous in Hmong villages. To our right, a one-room primary school overlooks the village. I can't resist peeking inside. The teacher sits at the back of the class as the students take turns reading aloud from a Lao text. They sit three or four abreast in tightly spaced rows, sharing long, slender wooden tables that serve as communal desks. It is hard to imagine studying all day in such a dimly lit classroom; the spaces between the wall siding boards and under the eaves provide the only light, as the village has no electricity.

Long and I leave some of our gear in the village chief's house and prepare for another hour of hiking to reach the slopes where the rice harvest is taking place. Our two companions decide to rest instead of coming with us. I take a moment to photograph an old woman who is making white pepper by hand. After soaking the pulp in a shallow pond, she dries it on wood-framed screens leaning against the side of her house. Later it will be ground with a mortar and pestle and used to season soups and boiled meats. Any surplus will be carried down the mountain and sold to vendors along Route Seven.

Long and I head south on a well-worn trail, passing many villagers who are already returning from the fields, some leading cattle or water buffaloes. Half an hour later we stop to photograph a young couple threshing their recently harvested rice crop. The man and his wife take turns threshing the rice while the other watches their toddler. They work under a crude lean-to structure, beating each bundle of rice stalks vigorously against a log suspended on two stakes about a foot off the ground. With each blow a few more rice kernels fall on the trampled earth. From time to time they are raked into a tall golden pile under the lean-to.

Shortly after we arrive, the young woman hands the baby to her husband and begins her shift. She picks up a fresh bundle of rice, swings it high over her head and behind her back, then brings it down on the log with all her might. She repeats this eight or nine times, removing about ninety percent of the rice kernels. Then she holds the bundle in one hand and beats it several times with a stick to extract the remaining kernels. The work is backbreaking and tedious, continuing ten hours a day until the entire year's crop has been threshed. I photograph the woman as she swings bundle after bundle of rice against a blue backdrop of Annamite Mountains. Her work will continue long after I leave. The baby has fallen asleep on a bed of spent rice stalks.

Continuing south along the trail, we enter a lush forest where an ancient stone jar site has recently been discovered by Western archeologists (though long known to local Hmong villagers). Only a few yards off the trail we begin to spot the two-thousand-year-old lichen-encrusted vessels half-hidden under foliage and nestled against tree trunks. The jars in this grouping average four feet high and three feet in diameter. Occasionally we find a broken lid half-buried on the forest floor. One bigger-than-average jar boasts a strangling tree with octopus-like roots growing over the top of it. Found in isolated locations throughout northern Laos, the original purpose of these jars is a mystery. Some scholars speculate that they might have been used to store grain or spirits, but many questions remain unanswered about the identity of their makers and the source of the labor required to quarry and transport the stone. Our brief detour to explore the jars provides a welcome respite from the long hours of hiking we have already put in. As we walk through the forest it feels as though we are discovering them for the first time.

After leaving the forest, the trail cuts across increasingly steep hillsides scarred by the slash-and-burn agriculture of the Hmong. In every direction, massive charred tree trunks litter the terrain, surrounded by parched golden rice stubble sprouting from fire-blackened earth. Every year after the harvest, the Hmong set new swaths of mountainous

terrain ablaze to clear the land for planting next year's crop. This ancient farming method quickly exhausts the soil and results in a net loss of hardwood trees every year. Moreover, it is far less productive than the wet paddy farming practiced by the Lowland Lao. However, as relative newcomers to Laos—the Hmong only began to migrate here from southern China less than two hundred years ago—they must make do with the land no one else wants, just as they did for thousands of years as a minority culture in China.

Descending a long ridge, we come to a small plateau used by a Hmong family as a base camp to harvest their rice crop from the adjacent slopes. They have erected a small shelter where meals are taken and where the children who are old enough to be left unattended but too young to work spend their days. A beautifully arranged wheel of

strand of rice cinched around its girth and then left to dry on the hillside. The work crew includes two brothers, their aging mother, and their two young wives, each carrying a baby on her back. While the others cut rice, one brother gathers up the tied bundles from the hillside, carries them back to the plateau, and arranges them on the growing dome.

After getting some telephoto shots from the relative comfort of the plateau, I decide to brave the steep slope myself, in order to capture close-up images of the workers. I descend a steep ravine, using a charred tree trunk to get across to the wall of rice on the other side. Once there, I find it almost impossible to keep my balance with the heavy camera and lenses dangling from my neck. I slowly make my way toward the workers, grasping handfuls of rice stubble to keep from falling. These farmers move surprisingly fast considering the difficulty of the terrain; I can barely keep up with them. I try to anticipate their movements and then position myself a little bit ahead, photographing them as they approach, but it is easier said than done; my footholds often give out and I am soon covered with the black soot of the scorched hillside. I photograph the two young women, aged seventeen and eighteen, and marvel at their ability to work all day under these grueling conditions and still keep their balance while carrying babies on their backs. Suddenly the old woman working a few yards up the slope loses her footing, slides, and crashes into me; together we slide a dozen more yards down the dusty

rice bundles some fifteen feet in diameter and about three feet high is slowly taking shape. It will eventually rise to a golden dome resembling one of Monet's haystacks. Once harvested, the rice must dry in this formation for a week or more before it can be threshed.

From the edge of the small plateau I photograph the family cutting and bundling rice on a near-vertical wall of mountainside. They move slowly across the slope, balancing on precarious footholds as they cut the stalks with small hand scythes. Each bundle is tied with a single

hillside as everyone else breaks into hysterical laughter. After an hour of this punishment, I decide that I have enough pictures and retreat to the plateau, exhausted. It is almost incomprehensible to me how hard these people work to produce just enough rice to subsist on for a year. The statistics Americans are always being fed about how much work we supposedly do in a year shrivel to insignificance after spending a day with these Hmong farmers.

As the light in the sky grows dim, Long and I follow the family back to Ban Pha Keo. Along the way they gather large, heavy branches to cut up for firewood. It is dark by the time we get back to the village and the temperature is already dropping. Long and I relax in the home of the village chief as his wife kills a scrawny chicken and boils it for dinner. The chief's house is relatively large and well built; the cooking fire keeps it toasty warm. Long, who grew up in a similar village at lower altitude, complains to me in English about the meal: "The problem with these villagers is always the food. They don't know how to cook the way people in the city like to eat." I chuckle to myself at his condescending tone, knowing that he was raised on food exactly like what we are now eating. Although the chicken is tough and scrawny, the freshly ground white pepper lends both the meat and broth a delicious flavor. After a long, hard day of hiking and photography, this simple, hearty fare provides welcome sustenance. Even Long has to admit that the sticky rice has an unusually sweet, pungent flavor that comes from being so recently harvested.

A calm descends on the village as we finish eating and stare into the fire. The ambient sound bed of crickets, frogs, and cicadas lulls me into a soporific state. With no electric lighting, it is incredibly dark out; even the simplest errand is better postponed until morning. After a day so long and exhausting, it seems like two or three have passed since it began. I can think of nothing but sleep. But it is not to be. Just as I begin contemplating where I will lie down in the chief's warm, spacious house,

Long informs me that the family we photographed harvesting rice has invited me to come stay with them. It seems to me that there is plenty of room in the chief's house for both Long and me, since all of the children have already grown up and moved to the city, but before I get a chance to plead my case, the young father from the other family arrives with a flashlight and leads me to his much smaller, more crowded house.

Divided into two rooms, the rickety dwelling sits on short legs above the bumpy terrain on which it is built. Some of the village's homes are constructed in this nontraditional way, as the rocky, sloping mountain soil does not afford enough good sites to build standard, packed-earth Hmong houses. As a result, this stilted house is creaky, cold, and drafty.

The entire family sleeps in the back room so that I can have the single wooden palette in the front room to myself. By candlelight, I

arrange my body diagonally on the short, bumpy pallet, using a foul-smelling blanket as a makeshift mattress and piling all of my extra clothes on top of me for warmth. I blow out the candle and am plunged into a total darkness to which I am unaccustomed. Within a few minutes, the formerly peaceful village comes alive with a loud cacophony of human and animal noises that will last most of the night. Eventually the human noises subside, but it hardly makes any difference in the overall chorus of squawking chickens, crowing roosters, grunting or squealing pigs, fighting dogs and cats, and the occasional bellow of a water buffalo. Add to this the close-range sounds of snoring family members, babies who wake up and cry at all hours, a dozen people crowded into a small wooden house, and a pallet built for someone five feet tall, and you have a foolproof recipe for *falang* insomnia.

I toss and turn for what seems like an eternity, searching for a comfortable position that does not exist. Finally I begin to discern a grid of dawn sky leaking through the gaps in the roof. The young mother is the first one to get up, building a cooking fire in the adjacent kitchen. I join her and warm myself by the fire as she begins her daily chores. She starts a big pot of rice, then peels and chops squash, all while keeping an eye on her youngest toddler. As soon as she has a spare moment, she sweeps the kitchen floor and outer porch with a short-handled broom. Most of her work is done in a stooping or squatting position. Soon she will return to the vertical rice fields to put in another full day of harvesting while carrying the baby on her back. This mature eighteen-year-old seems worlds apart from her mall-hopping, text-messaging counterpart in the United States.

I prowl the village in the cold, bluish light of early dawn, hoping to capture images that might not be possible later in the day. An old man grinds corn using a wood and stone contraption that looks like it might have been designed by Rube Goldberg if he had lived two hundred years ago. Children slop hogs, feed cattle and chickens. Families breakfast on the same food they dined on the night before, fortifying themselves for another day of harvesting, threshing, or pounding their rice crops. In a few hours I will leave Ban Pha Keo, unlikely to ever return, but I will carry memories of this village and her people with me for the rest of my life. When I go home to the United States and visit my Hmong friends in their familiar houses and apartments, I will see them in an entirely new way.

LIFE AND DEATH
IN A HMONG VILLAGE

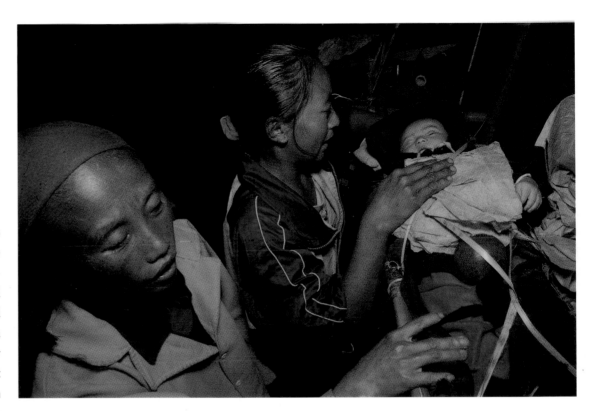

I twist a wide-angle lens onto my camera and step back so that I can frame the entire house in the background with a tall, spiny cactus in the foreground. This cactus is the last thing I had ever expected to photograph in monsoonal Laos, but I have learned to expect the unexpected ever since my first visit to a Hmong village, which required a two-day boat journey up the Mekong to an isolated bend in the river without any road access. As soon as I stepped ashore, a woman asked me if I would take a message to her relatives in the United States.

"Where do they live?" I asked.

"Fresno."

So today, in the hills of Xieng Khouang Province, my unlikely encounter with a cactus barely fazes me. It is the least of the surprises that await me in Ban Tha Chok.

Established more than a hundred years ago, Ban Tha Chok is one of the oldest extant Hmong villages in Laos. Its survival is something of a miracle given the heavy fighting along nearby Route Seven during both the First and Second Indochina Wars. Today, about eighty families live here in large wooden houses nestled among lush gardens, mature fruit trees, and thick stands of cultivated bamboo. Huge, fat pigs wander about everywhere, a testament to the relative wealth of the village.

Broad wooden yokes have been lashed to their shoulders in an attempt to prevent them from wriggling out of their pens, but many escape on a regular basis, feasting on neighbors' vegetable crops.

Long Vang and I stop to look at a house with a coffin resting ominously against one wall; he explains that someone in the family is expected to die soon. The simple hardwood casket is built entirely with joinery rather than nails, as the Hmong belief system does not permit the dead to be buried with any metal objects other than their silver jewelry.

We visit another house nearby where I photograph the high-ceilinged interior, with its upper-level loft and ornate shamanic altar. A fire smolders on the earthen floor, providing warmth against the high-altitude chill. Bright skylight oozes into the smoky atmosphere

through the open eaves and wide gaps in the wood siding. Later, Long tells me that Hmong teenagers often begin their earliest flirtations by whispering secret messages through these gaps in the walls.

War has altered the landscape of Ban Tha Chok village: American-made bomb casings are seen everywhere and pressed into service for many unlikely purposes. They are the legs that hold granaries above ground to keep vermin out of last year's rice and corn crops. Suspended horizontally on a pair of forked stakes, the half-shell casings serve as sinks for washing vegetables, pots, and pans. Filled with topsoil, they become herb and flower planters. Left empty on the ground, they are used to feed pigs. Some families anchor them side by side in the dirt to construct fences around their houses or gardens. The most impressive example of this at Ban Tha Chok is a fifty-foot-long fence built from matching six-foot bomb casings. At the house next door, an old woman sweeps detritus from her front walkway into a large dustbin pounded out of rusty war scrap; it still bears a faint U.S. Air Force insignia. Every family can tell a story about a relative who has been maimed or killed by unexploded ordinance.

Long and I walk up a hill where a knot of young men stand talking among themselves. After a brief exchange with them, Long turns to me and says, "You're in luck; there is a funeral today." They point us toward the very last house at the end of a path where the village peters out at the foot of a mountain. As we approach, I hear the beat of a drum and the low wheezing sounds of a *qeej*. An inebriated man emerges from the open doorway and greets us. Long asks him if I can photograph the funeral. Without uttering any response, the man grabs me by the arm and pulls me into the dark, smoky house. After my eyes adjust, I see two young women standing over the body of a small baby resting on a pallet of bamboo lashed together in the shape of a boat. The structure is anchored to the back wall of the house with two lengths of twine at about shoulder height to the mourners. Dressed in a bright red hooded jumpsuit and swaddled with ceremonial cloth and paper, the body of the infant is tightly bound to the boat-shaped pallet, which the Hmong believe will carry the soul to its next destination: the Land of Darkness, where the *dab* and *neeb* live. A large orange tucked against the body and a bottle of rice whiskey hanging beneath the palette provide sustenance for the journey.

The drunken man hurries me over to the mourners, who immediately turn to pose for mug shots in front of the corpse. Mounting a flash on my camera, I oblige them. The older of two sisters is the mother of the deceased baby. After the mug shots are finished, the women return to their mourning and I am free to begin capturing the funeral as it unfolds. The two sisters lean against the pallet, stroking the dead infant and crying theatrically. Behind them, a man sets two large piles of spirit money aflame on the packed-earth floor, momentarily bathing all of the participants in an orange glow. Two *qeej* players prowl for *dab*, crouching low and wheeling about in slow circles to the steady beat of the drum. Family members squat along the walls of the house; others wander about, carrying open bottles of *lao lao*, or rice whiskey. Two older women join the younger ones in front of the pallet, adding their more experienced voices to the collective wailing. As successive piles of spirit money are burned, ashes accumulate in the mourners' hair. The smoke thickens, the beat of the drum grows louder, the wheezing *qeej* players spin like whirling dervishes, the wailing of the mourners rises, the atmosphere in the house is charged.

Even though gaining access to this funeral was easy, it poses formidable technical challenges for photography. The house is pitch dark inside, while the tropical daylight seeping through the doorway, eaves, and gaps in the walls is blindingly overexposed. Whenever a pile of spirit money is burned, the surroundings are illuminated for a few brief seconds before the flimsy tissue turns to ash. Using an electronic flash is always a photographer's last resort; it creates glary, intrusive lighting, like poking a flashlight in someone's face. Setting up my tripod, I experiment with a variety of slow exposures, transforming the participants into blurry, silhouetted ghosts as they move across my frame. I add a little flash to the mixture, lighting only the foreground and creating a stop-time image in the midst of a blur. The result is a frightening and somewhat distorted picture that comes closer to capturing the spirit-laden ambience of the scene than a conventional exposure would.

Finally I pick up my tripod and move in close to the baby, focusing my wide-angle lens on its shriveled face, blue-white skin, and one tiny, stiff hand that protrudes from the swaddling. Sunlight bleeds through the gaps in the wall behind the baby; it is so far beyond the camera's exposure range that it casts halos around everything it touches. The mourners caress the body of the infant as I make several long exposures, transforming their hands into ghostly apparitions.

Overwhelmed by the smoke and the intensity of it all, I seek fresh air outside the house. About thirty men from the extended family are gathered around a long wooden table drinking *lao lao*. They have been drinking for hours, knocking back shots or guzzling the deceptively clear liquid from tall water glasses. By now, many are well on their way to passing out. The mood is more somber than festive. Every time a family member makes a cash contribution to the funeral or brings another bottle of whiskey, a tall, craggy-faced man stands and gives a short, solemn speech acknowledging the contribution, then duly records it in a notebook. Everyone in the assembled congregation echoes his blessing by downing another shot of *lao lao*. Occasionally, several men dare another to swallow a brimming glassful in a single draft; about half of it ends up dribbling down the front of his shirt.

I mount a close-up lens on my camera to make portraits of the

CIA secretly armed and funded Hmong insurgents in Laos as recently as 2004. I raise the camera to my eye and snap the drunken man's picture: he is framed perfectly between two bomb casings planted in the earth at about his height.

Exhausted from the funeral and hours of walking through the sprawling village, Long and I finally assent to a shot of rice whiskey apiece before heading off to eat lunch with the family of Xai, one of Long's high school classmates. As it turns out, Xai's sister, Nee, is the mother of the deceased infant; she has also taken a break from mourning at the funeral to come home for lunch. As Xai's mother kills and plucks a chicken, we sit around the fire, talking. I

men's faces. A partially overcast sky veils the midday sun, creating soft light. The men are remarkably easy to photograph in their inebriated state. It is almost as if they are sleeping; the muscles in their faces are completely relaxed, allowing the character of each man to show through. I walk around the table photographing them one at a time. Each face has its own particular pathos—a crooked jaw, a wandering eye, lines of age and worry. I try to imagine each man's inner thoughts and the arc of his life story, but the chasm of language and experience that separates us is too deep.

A small, wiry man in his thirties approaches me, aggressively beating his chest and exclaiming "CIA" over and over. He is far too young to have fought in the war, yet he appears to be trying to convince me that he has some connection with the agency. Rumors persist that the

learn that the dead baby is Nee's seventh child; she is twenty-four and has been married for nine years. A gaunt, dark-skinned girl with a pronounced overbite, her brow is already permanently creased with worry. However, at her mother's home she seems more relaxed than she did at the funeral. After lunch we all pose together for mug shots and, for the first time, Nee smiles.

It is four o'clock and only a couple of hours remain before sundown; the light is at its best now, and not to be wasted. I am offered the choice of either going to watch a soccer game or visiting the well at the far end of the village. I choose the latter, knowing that at this time of day the well is always the hub of village life. As we walk down the sloping path, kids trudge past us hauling twin pails of water balanced over their shoulders on bamboo sticks. Women wrapped in sarongs pass us going both ways, carrying buckets with soap, shampoo, and toothbrushes. An old man leads his buffalo by the ring in its nose.

At the end of the trail, we reach a big muddy area bustling with activity. Villagers wade through the ankle-deep muck to fill their buckets for cooking, drinking, and watering vegetable gardens. A group of women and children stand on a small slab of concrete, pouring bowls of water over themselves, scrubbing their hair, and brushing their teeth; bathing is, by necessity, a public act in most Laotian villages.

Nearby, three women squat on slightly higher ground, doing their laundry by hand. An obese pig wallows in the mire. The old man we passed earlier on the trail rolls up his pants legs and leads his buffalo to drink. At the heart of all this muddy chaos lies the secret to Ban Tha Chok's longevity and prosperity: a deep natural spring that has given life to the village for more than a century. As day turns to dusk, I am reminded that the life-giving power of water is more enduring than the destruction of war.

XYOO TSHIAB/NEW YEAR

Two women kneel on the asphalt selling medicinal herbs, their goblin-shaped roots and dried mushrooms spread out on a pair of small ground cloths. Less than fifty yards away, a high-tech vendor under a tent is selling the latest Hmong Hotties pinup calendar and showing "modeling" videos of scantily-clad Hmong co-eds straddling Harley-Davidsons, primping for the camera or frolicking by the shore of a Midwestern lake. Thousands of Hmong in traditional New Year costumes stroll the fairgrounds, filling the crisp December air with the exquisite sound of millions of jingling silver coins. Meanwhile, loudspeakers blast Hmong pop music in several conflicting keys, punctuated by frequent blaring announcements from the main stage. There, a new Miss Hmong will be crowned and General Vang Pao will give the same speech he gave the year before about Hmong solidarity and the importance of education.

Nowhere is the jarring fusion of Hmong and American cultures more in evidence than at Fresno's Hmong New Year Festival, the largest celebration in the Diaspora. Each day, approximately twenty thousand Hmong from all over the world converge on the city's sprawling fairgrounds, feasting on barbecued pork, yellow saffron chicken, purple sticky rice, and green papaya salad. Vendors sell Hmong movies, music, and books, traditional and modern clothing, shamanic accoutrements, musical instruments, karaoke systems, and more. Itinerant photographers shoot portraits in makeshift tent studios painted with scenes of the CIA landing strip at Long Cheng. Small armies of amateur videographers record anything and everything in seemingly endless takes; later the tapes will be dutifully labeled, placed on living room shelves, and rarely, if ever, watched.

In most Hmong American households, the living room shelves are also lined with dozens of commercially produced Hmong-language movies, high melodramas shot on impossibly low budgets. Filmed

Liquid Lounge, a Hmong-owned nightclub in Fresno.

with handheld video cameras and rudimentary lighting, the feature-length stories combine traditional elements of Hmong culture—such as bride kidnapping and soul loss—with B-movie plot devices and the ethos of pop culture. What the actors lack in experience they make up for with passion and energy. This rich fusion of Hmong folklore with traditional and pop culture represents an as yet untapped goldmine for cultural anthropologists and world cinema buffs alike. Their potential is not lost on Hmong New Year vendors, however, who sell thousands of DVDs every day of the festival. Meanwhile, the Hmong movie industry is beginning to mature with some higher-budget productions shot on 35mm film in Thai studios.

One mainstay of Hmong New Year remains relatively little-changed in America: *pov pob*, the ball-toss courtship game. At any given hour, hundreds of young men and women stand facing each other in long rows across a wide expanse of asphalt at the center of the fairgrounds. In an updated version of a centuries-old ritual, they lob fluorescent green tennis balls back and forth while making small talk. Traditionally, the New Year celebration follows the end of the harvest season, when young people from isolated mountain villages come together to find marriage partners. Fresno's Hmong New Year fulfills the same function on a global scale, bringing potential mates together from the far corners of the Diaspora: Alaska, Australia, France, Minnesota, China, North Carolina, Laos, Vietnam, Wisconsin, Arkansas, and Thailand. There is even a section of the concourse reserved for widows and widowers, who come to toss the ball in hopes of remarrying. The winter celebration, which occupies the week bridging Christmas and New Year's Day, is always followed by a spate of February and March weddings.

When a Hmong couple begins to take more than a passing interest in one another, they often play a variation of the *pov pob* game in which one player must surrender an item of clothing to the other if he or she drops the ball. Given the many accoutrements and layers of clothing that make up a traditional New Year costume, the game can go on indefinitely. I photograph one young couple engaged in a match so lengthy that it draws a large crowd. The young man appears to be winning, as the young woman coyly drops ball after ball, giving up her purse, parasol, and bonnet. Once the easy stuff is gone, she starts handing over her jewelry, piece by piece. Her shoes come next, surrendered one at a time. At this point the young man begins letting her win back an item now and then in order to prolong the game. He gives her back a single shoe, forcing her to limp awkwardly on one high heel and one bare foot, which she manages with flirtatious grace. Later in the evening, the pair will undoubtedly attend one of the many disco-style New Year parties held in the fairgrounds' exhibition halls or in Southeast Fresno's Asian nightclubs. There, live bands and DJs will play all-night sets of Thai-style pop music with Hmong lyrics.

Wanting to discover the traditional roots of Hmong New Year, I fly to Phonsavan, the new capital of Xieng Khouang Province, near the Plain of Jars. Before boarding my plane in Vientiane, I phone Long Vang to let him know my arrival time. "The airport here is full of Hmong girls," he informs me, referring to a recent plot twist in the evolving refugee saga. Following the death of Lao communist party ideologues Kaisone Pomvihane and former Prince Souphanavong in the early 1990s, the new government embarked on a slow path of liberal reform, opening the country to tourism for the first time since 1975. Eventually, it even became possible for some Hmong American refugees to return to Laos as tourists. In addition to many families who come to celebrate the New Year with their relatives in the homeland, some Hmong American men leave their families at home and come to Xieng Khouang alone to look for a second wife. "We have a saying," Long tells me. "Old bulls eat young grass." Paying bride prices many times higher than the local rate of three million Lao *kip* (about $350), these old bulls go on shopping-spree honeymoons with their teenage brides for several weeks. When it comes time to return to work and family in the United States, a tearful drama is played out again and again at the Xieng Khouang airport. The men promise to come back soon or to send for their new brides just as soon as the visa paperwork comes through, but most of the girls end up abandoned at the airport with shopping bags full of new clothes.

By the end of the war, the former provincial capital of Xieng Khouang

Hmong New Year in Phonsavan.

Town had become uninhabitable due to the prevalence of unexploded ordinance, so a new capital was established thirty kilometers away in a sleepy village called Phonsavan. Today the town is about as bustling as a Lao provincial capital gets; several blocks near the confluence of its two major roads are cluttered with two-story buildings, while motorbike traffic putts lazily through its streets. As tourism continues its steady growth, signs of a new prosperity are seen everywhere. Lao McMansions costing twenty or thirty thousand dollars to build are sprouting up like weeds within a five-mile radius. These two-story brick and concrete dwellings with their red tile roofs and gaudy banisters evoke the cul-de-sac palaces that have sprawled over California's landscape during the last quarter-century. Even more incongruous is Phonsavan's new three-story *talat* or central market, a strange-looking fusion of a traditional Lao market, a modern Chinese temple, and a San Diego shopping mall. A first-time visitor to Phonsavan would never suspect that the town acquired electricity only five years ago.

Phonsavan's Hmong New Year Festival, held on an old landing strip built by the French and later used by the CIA, is an immediate disappointment. With the advent of electricity and tourism, all the commercial trappings of American Hmong New Year have arrived ahead of me: blaring loudspeakers, carnival rides, and vendors galore. Hmong American videographers record everything in endless detail. There are subtle differences, however. The New Year *hu plig* ceremonies in Hmong homes are still very traditional. Among the ball tossers, one finds many talented young singers who are still able to memorize the long narrative New Year songs now rarely heard in America. Whenever a particularly gifted vocalist breaks into an ancient song, he or she is quickly surrounded by a bevy of Hmong American videographers who, dressed in leather jackets and pointing handheld cameras, resemble undercover cops making a bust. Meanwhile, in the dry, brown hills on the outskirts of town, the centuries-old tradition of Hmong bullfighting draws big crowds.

Compared with the Spanish version of the sport, Hmong bullfighting is surprisingly humane, even tame. Here the bulls fight each other, rather than being ritually killed by a matador and his picadors, as they are in Spain. Bred specifically for fighting, the muscular animals sport tall Brahman humps, long midsections, and curved horns. Yet they are surprisingly reluctant to fight. By my count, seven out of every ten pairs of bulls introduced to each other in the big open field fail to even tussle, wandering disinterestedly apart, despite the goading of their handlers. Spectators must sometimes wait an hour or more before two bulls finally take sufficient offense to one another and lock horns. When they do, a collective gasp sweeps through the crowd and all eyes are fixed on the dueling pair. The drama is usually over in a few minutes, when the stronger bull chases the weaker off the field without any major injury. Half a dozen handlers wielding tall bamboo poles scurry to block the bulls from running into the crowd, but they are not always successful.

Not satisfied in my quest to photograph Hmong New Year in its more traditional form, I make plans with Long Vang to visit the remote villages of Xam Neua District, in Houaphan Province, to the northeast. Every year the clan leaders of each region meet to decide when the New Year celebration will start, based on the harvest schedule. Because of the delayed harvest at Xam Neua's considerably higher altitude, we still have a few days before the festivities will begin there. The mostly uphill journey takes us two days in a four-wheel-drive vehicle. We see little traffic along desolate Route Six, which twists and turns northeast through a steep alpine landscape. Along the way, we scout villages representing several of the eight Hmong tribes, predominantly Black, Green, and White—each tribe recognizable by its distinct costume and dialect. Some villages are perched precariously on high ridges while others straggle along the road. A few are hidden from view.

Despite the isolation we encounter today, Xam Neua District saw a lot of action during the war; some villages supported the communists while others fought for Vang Pao and the CIA. The district was strategically important to the North Vietnamese, who used its tangled network of mountain paths and roads known as the Ho Chi Minh Trail to move supplies south. Meanwhile, their Pathet Lao allies had established headquarters fifty miles northeast in the giant caves of Vieng Xai, which sheltered them from American bombs. Vang Pao's greatly outnumbered forces sought to disrupt Vietnamese supply lines and slow the Pathet Lao's inevitable southward expansion.

Today it is hard to tell which villages supported which side; only the elders know, and they are careful about what they say. Those too young to remember are occupied with preparations for New Year. Young men take turns pounding sticky rice into a doughy confection with hand-hewn wooden mallets. Young women shape the dough into patties and wrap them in banana leaves. Children jump up and down on split-open tree branches while others feed lengths of sugarcane through the gap to squeeze the juice out. Later they will boil it down to make molasses-tasting candy. Any young women who have not yet finished their New Year costumes are busy sewing in order to be ready for the big day.

After traversing the highest mountains in the Province, we descend into a narrow river valley that is home to Xam Neua Town. The sun has set and it is already getting cold by the time we find a guesthouse. The concept of a heated building is unknown in Laos, so I ask for two extra blankets. Donning every layer of clothing I have with me, I climb under my three blankets and wrap my polar fleece jacket around my head. Reading by flashlight, I notice my breath becoming visible. By the time I awaken at 5:00 a.m. I am too cold to stay in bed, so I get up

On the steep climb out of Xam Neua Town, dense fog obscures the winding road and slows our progress. After another hour of zigzagging switchbacks, the sun begins to break through. We round a steep curve near the summit of a mountain and suddenly we are above the mist. I jump out of the truck to photograph the incredible view. Distant peaks rise above us like tropical islands in a vast sea of white that stretches to the horizon. Below us, the mist fills deep ravines, turning jagged ridges into floating mirages. Slow-motion waves of white lap at the mile-high shoreline, hiding one ridge while revealing another. The crystalline blue sky and thin mountain air make me giddy as I greedily snap frame after frame of the amazing scene. I feel like I have found the mythical Hmong homeland, Ntuj Khiab Haub, or at least the top of the world.

A short while later, we round a bend and stumble on yet another amazing scene: scores of Hmong youth line both sides of the road dressed in striking black and blue costumes. Dozens of balls fill the air, flying so rapidly in such high arcs that they seem like thousands. The sky virtually boils with them. The balls are hand-wound from long strips of black cloth, a labor of love; no one in these parts has ever seen a fluorescent green Wilson. The skill of the players is markedly superior

and go outside. It is pitch black and the temperature is zero degrees Celsius. I had hoped to find hot food or drink in a café, but nothing is open yet, so I jog around the perimeter of the shuttered central market to keep warm. After several laps, an early-bird market vendor shows up and lights a small fire. He is soon joined by several colleagues and a tall, shivering *falang*, who huddle together in silence around the modest blaze.

As dawn breaks, I decide to wake Long and the driver so that we can get an early start. Every morning, a beautiful mist enshrouds the mountains, then quickly dissolves as the sun rises. So far, I have not managed to photograph it successfully. Today's plan is to retrace yesterday's route, revisiting the most interesting villages as New Year festivities begin.

to that seen at lower elevations, where the participants stand but a few feet apart on flat ground. By contrast, these mountain-born teenagers effortlessly toss the black orbs thirty feet across the road and catch them with the confidence of seasoned outfielders. Route Six sees so little traffic in a day that their play is scarcely ever interrupted.

The feeling of joy in the air is palpable on this first day of New Year. I have never seen anything like it in California. These villagers depend on rice farming for their survival. Their entire year is planned according to its cycles: clearing the land, planting, harvesting, drying, threshing, and pounding the rice. Once all of this work is done, they have earned some well-deserved time off to focus on other aspects of their lives—family, spiritual practice, celebration, games, courtship and marriage. All year long they look forward to New Year, especially the teenagers in isolated villages who must work every day and do not have time to go look for eligible marriage partners from other clans. When the rainy season ends and the first day of New Year finally arrives under blue skies, a buzz of jubilant excitement is seen, heard, and felt everywhere in the mountains of Xam Neua. Meanwhile, in central California, December brings gray, drizzly weather. Everyone gets up in the morning and goes to their jobs just as they do every other day. The dates set aside for New Year celebrations are merely arbitrary ones, based more on facility rental schedules than the agrarian past that is quickly vanishing from the collective Hmong American memory.

With some reluctance I leave this Black Hmong village behind to explore others along the road. We pass many villages celebrating on a smaller scale, some with as few as ten or fifteen ballplayers. Finally we stop at Ban Mone, a large White Hmong village spread out over a broad slope overlooking a small valley; the superiority of its flat bottom land for rice growing explains the size and prosperity of the village. Many of the wooden houses here have fenced enclosures for livestock, including a few of the rarely seen Hmong ponies. Long asks some kids to take us to the village cemetery. My anticipation soon turns to disappointment, though: not only is there nothing to photograph but there is almost no discernable sign that the overgrown knoll is actually a burial ground. Two centuries of grave robbing by Chinese marauders have taught the Hmong to make their cemeteries as invisible as possible to outsiders.

Back in the village's central dirt area—its square, so to speak—about twenty young women in White Hmong costumes toss the ball, hoping that some young men from other villages will come to join them. Long finds it puzzling that none have arrived yet, given the relative wealth of the village and the beauty of the women. We visit a house where an old woman is busy brewing a huge kettle of *lao lao* (rice whiskey) over a fire. She places a shot glass at the end of a long, thin spout and turns the spigot. The trickle is so slow that it takes about a minute to fill the glass. The warm brew surprises my wary palate; it is sweet, fragrant, and smoother than the finest saké. Although the sun is straight up in the sky, I cannot resist a second shot and then a third.

Suddenly, we hear an awful squealing sound outside. Three men have wrestled a pig onto its side and are binding its feet together with leather lanyards. As if the pig possesses some ancestral knowledge of its role in the impending *ua neng* ceremony, it screams its lungs out and gives its handlers a run for their money. The squealing continues even after they bind the pig's snout. In a nearby house, the preliminary *hu plig* portion of the ceremony is about to begin. The shaman, a small, wiry man with large, bulging eyes, picks up a live chicken and stands in the back doorway of the house facing out. For half an hour he calls the soul in long, musical tones and waves the chicken around. Next he lays his spirit rattle on the floor and tosses two pairs of split water buffalo horns into its foot-wide hoop. If the horns land with their flat

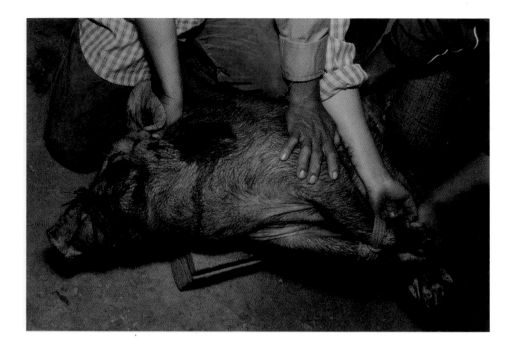

except for shiny blue cuffs on his shirt sleeves, the shaman performs a ceremony that is nearly identical to the ones I have seen in Fresno. Instead of watching TV, however, the family members all sit in rapt attention, focused on the shaman.

After the boy is untied, he gets up from the bench and rejoins his family. The shaman lowers his hood and begins the spirit trance. The head of the household stands behind him, holding the shaman's waist as he leaps energetically on and off the bench. I recognize some of his vocal sounds, having heard them many times in California. In particular, there is a whooping tongue trill that I hear at every ceremony, regardless of the shaman's gender. After the Xam Neua shaman emerges from his hour-long trance, it is time to kill the pig. This is done on the floor of the house without moving the animal from its ceremonial position. Three men hold the pig while a forth slits its throat with a long, sharp knife. A large bowl is placed under the fatal wound to collect the blood, much of which ends up on the dirt floor and splattered all over the men's pants legs. Gradually, the men relax their grip as the life flows out of the pig.

The entire house is suddenly abuzz with preparations for the meal. The now-limp pig is taken outside and rendered in a big black pot over a crackling fire. Two teenage girls are assigned the duty of killing the ceremonial chickens. Sitting cross-legged on the floor, one holds the feet and wings while the other pulls the head away from the body and slits the bird's throat; the chickens' blood is also collected for the meal. Women chop vegetables and boil sticky rice, tossing large balls of it in woven baskets to attain the desired consistency. Two older men sit in the corner, using lengths of plastic tubing to suck *lao lao* from a clay pot filled with fermenting purple rice. Finally, the feast is laid out on low wicker tables and everyone sits on the floor, eating from shared dishes. Egged on by several of the men, I try a spoonful of congealed pig's blood and quickly wash it down with *lao lao*.

sides up, it means that the sacrificial animal is ready to give its soul. If the horns land face down, it means that the shaman must wait and ask again. Normally the horns are thrown several times in rapid succession until they all land face up.

The basic setup for the *ua neeb* is similar to what I have photographed in California. The main difference is that here the pig will be kept alive during the first part of the ceremony. Since this family does not have an altar, a few shamanic accoutrements have been placed on a small table next to the wall. A teenage boy with persistent flu sits on a bench in front of the makeshift altar. The bound pig is carried in, still struggling and squealing, and is laid on the dirt floor behind him. A long ribbon of black cloth is tied around the pig's neck and then around the boy's waist. Clad entirely in black

After bidding the family farewell and wishing them a happy New Year, Long and I go looking for our driver, who is nowhere to be found. We follow the road from one end of the village to the other with no luck. Along the way, we stumble upon the largest piece of war ordinance either of us has ever seen. Nearly twenty feet long, the crumpled missile resembles a crashed passenger jet without wings lying by the side of the road. Finished in glossy white enamel, the mysterious craft still sports a red-white-and-blue U.S. Air Force insignia on its tail fin. While I am busy photographing it from half a dozen different angles, Long finally reaches our driver on his cell phone and he soon arrives to pick us up. A month later, as I sit editing my images in a Bangkok hotel room, the pictures of the missile somehow disappear. I am looking at them one morning, and a few hours later they are gone. I search every folder of images from the trip three times, but the phantom ordinance never reappears.

Our next stop is Ban Nong Oun, a large Green Hmong village where bullfights are taking place. The day's events draw hundreds of spectators from many other villages. With everyone dressed in tribal costumes, the crowd is as much an attraction as the bullfighting. The dusty contest is staged in the village's bowl-like central field; its houses are scattered over the surrounding hillsides and ridges. Spectators line the road, sit elbow to elbow on livestock fences, and even perch on rooftops to get a clear view of the action. A few brave souls meander about in the field with the handlers for a closer look; not infrequently, they become part of the spectacle when the scuffling bulls force them to scatter and run. As usual, some of the bulls refuse to fight, but enough of them butt heads to make the long walk worthwhile for visiting villagers.

After several bullfights, a pair of water buffaloes is led onto the field. A shudder of excitement sweeps through the crowd. Larger and heavier than fighting bulls by several hundred pounds, water buffalo bulls are also stronger, faster, and meaner. When the pair is introduced

bull. My zoom lens captures the fur on its forehead, scraped raw and bleeding. Time slows and a strange sense of calm overcomes me; I feel as though I have all the time in the world to get the picture just right, clicking off one minor variation after another. Then, with an abrupt motion, my perfect frame suddenly disintegrates and I feel the beat of heavy hooves at very close range. A surge of adrenaline propels me as I turn and run the opposite direction. Not daring to look back, I simply follow the handlers who are running ahead of me as fast as they can.

Once I reach a safe distance, I turn and watch as the larger buffalo concedes the contest by bolting in the opposite direction. With the victor in hot pursuit, the two crash into a vegetable garden, taking out a small fence. The handlers run around the backside of the garden to head them off, pounding the earth with their tall bamboo poles. The buffaloes wheel about, inflicting substantial crop damage, and run back into the makeshift arena. Without pausing, they head full speed toward the road. The crowd scatters and at least a hundred spectators who had been sitting on the five-foot-high roadside embankment all jump off at the same time. The buffaloes charge up the embankment and plow through a group of bystanders who do not move out of their way fast enough. A man carrying a baby on his back is knocked down, tumbling beneath eight galloping hooves. Miraculously, neither man nor baby is harmed. The buffaloes run down the road and disappear from sight, leaving their handlers in a cloud of dust.

We spend the night at Ban Nong Oun and set off in the morning to look for Ban Long Ang, a remote Black Hmong village that we'd heard about a day earlier. The village is not visible from the road, so we must look for a charred tree trunk on our left and then follow a dirt track. I am skeptical about these vague instructions but willing to take a chance. An hour later, the scene materializes, just as described. Shifting into four-wheel-drive, our driver negotiates the treacherous path,

there is no hesitation: they immediately lock horns and begin pushing each other with a G-force not seen on the field all day. Occasionally they break apart, scuffle, and collide with a bone-on-bone impact that is audible even over the din of the raucous crowd. I decide to go around to the opposite side of the field and squeeze through the crowd for some closer shots. By now, the buffalo bulls are locked in a head-to-head stalemate, thousands of pounds of pressure from each side holding the other in check. Soaked with sweat and breathing heavily, both animals are bleeding from head and neck wounds. I can't resist going in for some quick close-ups. I run a few yards closer to the pair, snap a few frames, then run closer still. Finally I move all the way in, squatting close to the ground and filling my frame with the faces of the enraged beasts. I can hear them exhaling as I focus on the crazed, glistening eye of the nearer deeply rutted from rainy season runoff and now dried hard as fired clay. We crawl along for a few hundred yards before the ups, downs, and ruts become too much for our vehicle. Long and I continue on foot, leaving our driver with the unenviable task of turning the truck around. Three hundred yards ahead, we reach the top of a ridge overlooking Ban Long Ang, whose thirty-six houses straggle down a steep slope. Rimmed with morning sunlight and set against a backdrop of smoke-blue mountains, the village couldn't be more picturesque. From our bird's-eye view we can see children in black tossing balls and hear the beat of a funeral drum.

As Long and I walk into the village, we cause an immediate stir. Men and women stare at us with a mixture of astonishment and laughter. Frightened children run into their houses and peer at us from doorways. Soon, nearly everyone in the village drops whatever they are doing to come gawk at us, or rather at *me*. "These villagers have never seen a *falang* before," Long whispers excitedly. The experience is also a first for him. Even the funeral mourners abandon their duty to come and stare at the white-skinned giant with green eyes, a floppy hat, and a huge black camera hanging around his neck. Now we are completely surrounded by a large crowd eagerly watching every move I make. They laugh hysterically whenever I raise the camera to my eye and take a picture. Parents push their shy kids to the front of the crowd for me to photograph them. Someone grabs me by the arm and drags me over to a corn grinding rig with a large circular stone. Urged on by their peers, two giggling women pretend to grind corn in order to have their photograph taken; the crowd roars with laughter as I oblige them.

Next I am escorted into the house where the funeral is taking place. The deceased, a twenty-one-year-old woman who succumbed yesterday to a long, debilitating illness, is laid out on a pallet in her New Year costume with a parasol suspended over her head. Her body is beginning

to swell with rigor mortis, and foam bubbles from her lips. Death came to this village on the first day of New Year.

After forty-five minutes, the novelty of my presence starts to wear off and the villagers return to their normal activities. Now I can do some real photography. I begin with the funeral, then wander around the village, making portraits. The faces of these people are extraordinary. Of all the Hmong I have encountered, they are the least touched by the outside world, living without electricity or motor vehicles, and possessing the fewest manufactured goods. I photograph a fortyish man dressed in everyday village black, standing uphill from me on a path. He has the face of an ancient warrior. With each click of the shutter I move a little closer, his intense gaze searing itself into my camera's memory chip. I photograph the faces of children whose shyness is beginning to wear off; they all have runny noses, due to the freezing nighttime temperatures. Some wear amulets around their necks, made from small gourds, animal bones, or teeth, to appease the spirits that cause sickness.

Long and I are invited into a house for lunch. A large family sits huddled around the fire, which, at this time of year, is kept perpetually lit. A black cooking pot and the rubber flip-flops everyone wears are the only signs of modernity. The menu consists of sticky rice and boiled greens. Predictably, Long complains about the lack of meat. I suggest that he add a bit of homemade pepper sauce to his greens; it is some of the best I have tasted. Unlike the Lao and Thai, who spice their food when they cook it, the Hmong prefer to serve their food unseasoned or lightly seasoned, with pepper sauce on the side. Homemade pepper sauce, with its endlessly delicious variations from family to family, is one of the highlights of every Hmong meal for me.

Very little conversation accompanies our lunch, as Long is having a difficult time understanding the village's dialect. After we finish eating, I move closer to the fire and reflect on my five-year journey in the Hmong Diaspora. Without a doubt, New Year in Xam Neua, and this village in particular, have been among the highlights. Yet as I look around the one-room dwelling, I feel hopelessly separated from its inhabitants by an insurmountable gulf of language and cultural disparity. I would need to live here for a year to really figure out what life in this village is all about. However, in less than an hour I will walk over the hill and drive back to civilization in my rented truck. What will I carry away, besides millions of ones and zeros stored on a memory chip?

My thoughts drift to my Hmong American friends at home. What do I really understand about them? I have shared their meals, ceremonies, funerals, weddings, even camping and hunting trips to the Sierra Nevada. I have listened to their stories and taken countless photographs.

I have had my own *hu plig* ceremony and been given a Hmong name. Yet, at some deep level, my Hmong friends remain a mystery to me. Suddenly I realize what it is that separates us: they are much more American than I am. With their strong commitment to marriage, family, fiscal discipline, and the practical matters of home life, the Hmong are one of the fastest assimilating immigrant groups ever thrown into the American melting pot. Meanwhile, here I sit, eight thousand miles from home, unmarried, without children, committed only to a life of arts, letters, and inquiry, living on unreliable income from grants, exhibitions, and book royalties. As my Hmong friends in California busily save for their children's college educations, I sit on a packed-earth floor in the mountains of Laos and seriously consider spending the next year of my life in this remote village.

When it comes time to leave, Long and I thank our hosts more with gestures than words. A crowd gathers for one more look at the unforgettable stranger who walked into their village on the second day of New Year, 2006. As I lift my camera to take a souvenir picture, I am seized with an epiphany: I see a crowd of Americans gathered around one of my photographs in a museum, gawking, pointing, and laughing, just as these villagers do now. I have a vision of photography as an imperfect two-way mirror, through which people from different cultures attempt to look at one another but, to a large extent, see only themselves. I wonder whether most Americans, without the benefit of an eight-thousand-mile trek to Xam Neua, five years of interviewing Hmong refugees, and five years of reading Hmong history and ethnography, can possibly grasp what they are seeing in a frozen frame of time. More important, I wonder if all of those prerequisites plus a camera make me any more qualified to tell this story than anyone else. In the end, viewers will have to ponder these questions for themselves, with only my mute color prints to guide them.

YER LOR LEE:
A HMONG SHAMAN
TELLS HER STORY

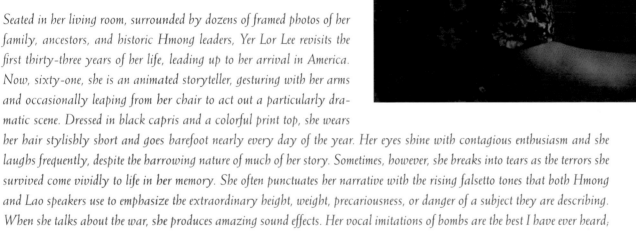

Seated in her living room, surrounded by dozens of framed photos of her family, ancestors, and historic Hmong leaders, Yer Lor Lee revisits the first thirty-three years of her life, leading up to her arrival in America. Now, sixty-one, she is an animated storyteller, gesturing with her arms and occasionally leaping from her chair to act out a particularly dramatic scene. Dressed in black capris and a colorful print top, she wears her hair stylishly short and goes barefoot nearly every day of the year. Her eyes shine with contagious enthusiasm and she laughs frequently, despite the harrowing nature of much of her story. Sometimes, however, she breaks into tears as the terrors she survived come vividly to life in her memory. She often punctuates her narrative with the rising falsetto tones that both Hmong and Lao speakers use to emphasize the extraordinary height, weight, precariousness, or danger of a subject they are describing. When she talks about the war, she produces amazing sound effects. Her vocal imitations of bombs are the best I have ever heard; she is a virtual audio catalog of falling ordinance, skillfully rendering both the trajectory and impact of each type of bomb.

The first thing I can remember is going hunting with my older brother, Za Teng. I was about three or four years old. He gave me a little basket to wear on my back; every time he shot a bird or a squirrel, he would put it in my basket. Za Teng was my favorite brother and I loved him very much. He was like a father to me because my own father had died when I was about a year old. Later, when the war came to Xieng Khouang, Za Teng was one of the first young men from our village to go fight and die.

Yer Lor as a child ca. 1940s, flanked by her mother, right, her grandmother, left, and three aunts.

My father had two wives, nine sons, and eight daughters; I am the youngest. All I can remember about my childhood is work. With our father gone, everyone had to work all of the time. When I was very young—too young to cut and bundle rice for the harvest—they would put a baby on my back and tie me to a tree stump with several other kids so we could not slip and fall down the steep hillsides where the rice grew. I would have to stay there all day and usually ended up falling asleep with the baby.

Without a husband, my mother had to do most of the farming and housework, with only her children to help. Besides that, she was the only shaman for our village of more than a hundred families. Once you become a shaman you have an obligation to help people when they come to you; you cannot refuse them. People came to our door at all hours of the night needing medicinal herbs, massages, or ceremonies. Mother was an expert on medicinal herbs, which not all shamans are, so she also served as the village doctor. She rarely slept more than two or three hours a night.

I was about eleven or twelve the first time I saw Vang Pao and the Americans. They came to build a base on the hilltop above our village. I remember how beautiful the parachutes looked floating in the sky as the airplanes dropped munitions. Soon after, the bombing started. I learned how to tell if a bomb was going to land close by or far away just by the sound it made. (*She demonstrates the difference.*) Even now, whenever I hear a loud noise of any kind, I get a sick feeling in my stomach and think about the war. All nine of my brothers had to go and fight, but only three came back. Today, I am very close to all of my siblings; we are more like best friends than brothers and sisters. Most Hmong families are close, but my siblings and I are even closer because of what we went through. We could never have survived without each other.

The war changed everything about our lives. We could not farm anymore and had to rely on American planes and helicopters to drop rice and other supplies. We used to grow a little opium on a plot of land high up in the mountains to sell to the Chinese traders who came every year. It took a whole day to walk up there and we had to sleep over. One night my mother put a dish of water out and in the morning it was frozen. I had never seen ice before! The Chinese traders paid us in silver, which we used to make the beautiful jewelry we wore around our necks. But once the war started, they stopped coming and the soldiers took over our land, so we no longer had any way to earn cash. From then on we had to move from place to place around the Plain of Jars, following the American rice drops. Every day the bodies of our village men arrived at the airport in Phonsavan. You could hear the weeping for miles.

I was fifteen when I married Wa. He was eighteen. Our marriage was arranged; my clan, the Lors, owed the Lees a daughter because my father, who was a Lor, had married my mother, who was a Lee. So I was chosen by the elders. I was very unhappy because I didn't like Wa when I first met him. Since he was too small to fight and had been sent home to guard his village, his elders decided that it was time for him to marry. That way he would have a wife to help him look after the village, which was a very small one with only six families. Just before the wedding, we had our photo taken together at a little studio in Xam Thong.

After we were married, I went to live in Wa's village for two years. I was miserable at first and thought about running away, but I knew that my family would only send me back. Wa's family was very poor—poorer than mine—and life in that village was very hard. I decided that I would work hard to pull the family up and, in a short time, I did. Soon our first daughter, Lo, was born. Shortly afterward, Wa left for Long Cheng to be trained as a military policeman. Two months later we all moved to a village near Xam Thong Airport, where Wa was stationed. For three years Xam Thong was relatively peaceful and we were able to settle down and begin raising our own family. My sons, Xeng and Xue (David) were born there.

Even though our marriage was arranged and even though I was against it at first, I learned to accept Wa as my husband and to love him. He is a good husband and has never taken a second wife, like some Hmong men did back then and some still do today.

The peace in Xam Thong did not last. When the fighting came too close to our village for comfort, everyone packed up to move, as we had done so many times before. As we headed along the trail toward what we hoped would be our next home, a small band of Pathet Lao soldiers ambushed us and started shooting. I ran as fast as I could but fell behind. Suddenly, my right hand was on fire; a second later the same fire exploded in my left leg and I fell. Pain filled my entire body as I lay in the dust, looking up at the sky and gasping for breath. It seemed like a long time passed before some men picked me up and carried me to a clearing, and then to the small medical clinic at Xam Thong Airport. I was operated on by a Filipino surgeon who had been hired by the Americans to take bullets out of their pilots. I limped around for almost two years before I could walk normally again. Even now, when the weather changes I still feel the pain.

As long as I live, I will never forget the day General Vang Pao left the country. People ran like the four rivers. Our village was total chaos. You'd see a Hmong family running along a path, carrying everything they had on their backs, and a short while later you would see another family running along the same path in the opposite direction. No one knew where to go or what to do next. Rumors swirled about the location of the Vietnamese soldiers, but no one really knew how far away they were. We only knew they were coming to kill us.

We decided to leave the village and hide in the jungle. I was still carrying Hli (Kristie) on my back; she was only a few weeks old. There were many loose bands of Hmong soldiers roaming the mountains with their families, hoping that General Vang Pao would come back and continue fighting. We heard about a massacre south of Vang Vieng at Hin Heup Bridge. Thousands of Hmong with no place else to go had gathered there and were trying to cross the bridge so they could continue south along the main road to Vientiane. Suddenly the Pathet Lao soldiers opened fire with mortars and rifles, killing some of the refugees and scattering the rest into the countryside. Wa's brother, Neng Thao, was there and made it back to tell us the story.

For the next few months we moved from place to place, mostly

Vang Vieng Valley, Laos .

was born—my arms and legs would become stiff and I would go into a kind of trance—but Yang's birth was different. I became far sicker than usual and stayed sick for almost a year. I was weak and delirious from almost constant fever. I suffered memory loss. Sometimes I had hiccups for days on end and could not eat. For a long time I could not even get up. Everyone thought I would die. When the rainy season finally came, it was the wettest one I can remember. It rained hard every day. Sometimes I would black out for hours at a time, then wake up to the sound of endless rain.

Finally, my family found a shaman who came to the house and performed a *ua neeb* ceremony for me. I lay on the ground because I was too weak to sit on the bench in front of the altar. When I heard the sound of the shaman's gong, I began to shake violently. The shaking became stronger and stronger, worse than any fever. Flashes of lightning lit up the room. I could hear loud claps of thunder and rain pounding the leaky thatch roof above me. Sometimes a droplet of rainwater would fall on me, cooling my burning face. I tried to focus my mind on the steady beat of the gong. As soon I started to shake, the shaman knew that a spirit had entered my body and that I was going to become a shaman myself. The shamanic spirit passes from generation to generation, looking for the right person. When it finds that person it will not let go until he or she becomes a shaman. I believe my mother's spirit passed to me that day.

The shaman told Wa and my cousin to help me up off the ground and onto the bench. As they did, the shaking became so strong that the two men could barely hold me. All of a sudden I started chanting; I didn't understand any of it, but it just kept coming out of me. I chanted for a long time and gradually stopped shaking. After the ceremony I recovered quickly. I started eating and soon became strong again.

The shaman who cured me became my mentor. He taught me about

hiding in the jungle. After the Hin Heup massacre, we knew that we had to stay off of the main roads. Our group consisted of twenty-four families from the Lee and Xiong clans, who were all related by marriage. We decided to work our way west through the mountains, toward the big valley north of Vang Vieng. The Pathet Lao had already cleared most of the Hmong population out of that area, so we were able to settle in an abandoned village with good land high in the mountains above the river. The village was situated far from the town of Vang Vieng, in a place so difficult to reach that the soldiers would be unlikely to find us. We lived peacefully there for about a year and a half.

My fifth daughter, Yang, was born in the hottest month of the dry season. I had always been sick for a few days after each of my children the spirit realm and showed me how to use the gong, saber, spirit rattle, split buffalo horns, dagger, finger bells, spirit money, eggs, rice, and other food offerings to negotiate with the *dab* for the return of a sick person's soul. It was an awkward situation, though, because he was a man. In our culture, if a married woman has any dealings with a man outside of her family, she must always go through her husband, who will then take care of the matter for her. She is not normally allowed to spend time with an unrelated man the way I did with that shaman. Since there was no female shaman in the village who could teach me, my family understood and accepted the situation.

People in the village soon began coming to see me about their problems and ailments, just like they do today. I remember one man who came to me because he had not been able to pee for several days. I asked him if he had put a nail in his altar recently. He said, "Yes, how did you know?" I told him that was the cause of his problem and sent him home to remove the nail. As soon as he pulled it out, he wet his pants! The altar has a soul—your soul. It is part of you, so when you put a nail in the altar it is like putting a nail in yourself.

When I go into a *ua neeb* or spirit trance, I cover my face with a cloth, so that my spirit mentor can instruct me in the proper *nkauj neej*, or ritual chants. If you remove the cloth, you won't be able to speak the language of the spirits, so you must keep it in place until the *ua neeb* is finished. There are two different types of shamans, those who wear a red cloth and those who wear a black one, as I do. Shamans who wear a red cloth keep the lightning guardian spirit, Xob, on their altar at all times and must therefore call upon him for every ceremony. Those who wear a black cloth only call upon Xob as a last resort, when negotiations with the *dab* have failed. The lightning guardian spirit is very powerful but can also be dangerous and unpredictable.

If there is a spirit in my presence when I enter the trance, I will see it right away. A spirit looks just like a human being. Sometimes there are more than one. When there are many spirits, the ceremony will be more difficult and take longer. If there are no spirits present, the ceremony will be finished quickly, but the patient's condition will not improve. During the ceremony there is a lot of conversing back and forth between the shaman and the spirits. The shaman relays the information back to the real world and then converses with the spirits again. That is why you hear so much talk mixed in with the chanting. There are many matters to be discussed; sometimes the ancestors bring up things that happened a long time ago and must be settled before the soul can be returned to its owner.

One full-moon night my children were out playing when two young men who had been assigned to guard the footpath to the village began to yell: "The Viet soldiers are coming!" These two were normally very quiet, so no one believed them at first until several gunshots rang out. We grabbed only the barest necessities and headed up the mountainside, where the thickest jungle lay. That night we lost some relatives who were not able to escape. For several days we moved through the jungle with the other survivors, wondering what to do next. The Vietnamese soldiers had us completely surrounded. The men had a meeting and discussed our options. If we surrendered as a group, the men and older boys would all be killed. If the women and smaller children surrendered, the men might be able to escape but would probably never see their families again.

After the men came back from the meeting everyone in our group began to cry uncontrollably. It seemed like there was really no way out. Some families decided to surrender, but my husband would never go along with such a plan. So we decided to leave the group and try to escape by ourselves. We met some Hmong people from Luang Prabang Province who hadn't fought in the war but still had to flee the communists and get out of the country. They decided to surrender, hoping for better treatment because their men had never been soldiers. They invited us to surrender with them, so my husband told them to go ahead, that we would follow after we rested a bit. Once they surrendered, the soldiers left, thinking they had captured all of the Hmong in the area, and we were able to move on.

The month that followed was the worst of our lives. We hid in the jungle northwest of Vang Vieng and foraged for food. The jungle in that area is so dense and tangled that almost no one lives there. We had only enough rice to cook one very small pot each morning. Each person got a handful and that was all we had to eat for the whole day. You never really know how good rice tastes until you have so little. The soldiers were constantly patrolling the area, so we had to be very quiet. My baby, Yang, cried a lot because I was not making enough milk and she was hungry. Her crying put everyone else at risk, so my husband dug a hole about eight feet deep; I would sit at the bottom of that hole with my baby to muffle the sound of her crying, so that the soldiers could not hear it. Sometimes I would have to sit down there in the dark for hours on end, breathing in the cold, dank smell of earth while the baby just cried and cried.

Finally our rice ran out. Everyone was hungry and there was nothing to eat anywhere in sight. Wa and David went out foraging all morning and came back in the afternoon with only a single small tuber that they had managed to dig up. It wouldn't even provide a mouthful for each person. Rain began to fall, softly at first, and then harder. I felt an anger well up in me just like I did when I first went to stay in my husband's village and saw how poorly everyone lived there. Somehow that anger, mixed with hunger, gave me the strength to go out and forage for food on my own. I wouldn't let anyone come with me. I moved quickly through the forest, barely caring if the soldiers heard me or not. I started digging near a large tree and found some fat, white tubers growing amongst its roots. I kept digging and soon had a basketful; they tasted like starchy yams if they were boiled long enough. We survived on them for the next few weeks.

The Vietnamese soldiers set up a base camp in our former village and began sending pro-communist Hmong every day to try to persuade us to surrender. Meanwhile they fired mortars and grenade launchers at us all night long. Some of them landed dangerously close. We lived in constant terror of being killed or captured at any moment. One night we heard the sounds of approaching footsteps and cracking branches. It was pitch dark and we had nowhere to run. As the sounds drew nearer I felt sick to my stomach. Everyone was sure we were going to die. Suddenly a man stepped into the clearing and we all let out a huge sigh of relief; it was only my brother-in-law, Lor Pao, who had come looking for us.

Lor Pao said it was safe to travel now and led us back to join the surviving members of our group, who had more food than we did. The men had a meeting and decided that we could not stay near Vang Vieng any longer. The time had come to begin moving south, toward the Mekong River and Thailand. But the journey might be dangerous, so we killed and boiled some chickens, then looked at their feet: the claws curled very nicely without crossing over one another, a sign that it was a good time to go. The journey would take about three months.

Along the way, we had to pass many villages. There were Lao, Hmong, Khmu, and other hill tribe people living in the area; many of these villagers had been neutral during the war, while others supported one side or the other. As we moved along through the hills and jungles, we had no way to know the difference, so we had to stay hidden by day and travel by night. Whenever we neared a village, we had to count on our luck. One day our luck ran out. Some men from our group went to

silver bars at the b
Song saw the sold
ground, just as I h
baskets got search
they ignored Song
who paused and g
When only a few
he moved on.

The next mor
us to the camp. B
diers had. They g
already come the
so they didn't wa
policeman pawed
buffalo horns, go
shaman in Vang
these things, som

The ride to E
able; we were pac
had to stand up t
tall barbed-wire f
markets were, th
near the open lat
week before we v
whole family live
felt so embarrass
Western-style cl
clothes that, by

In spite of th
For the first time

buy a couple of pigs from a Hmong village and brought them back to be cooked. They didn't know that the Hmong people who sold them the pigs were helping the communists. Soon the Vietnamese soldiers came and captured most of our group. They took us back to the village and left us in the custody of their Hmong collaborators.

Even though we were now prisoners of war, we considered our-selves fortunate that we were being held in a Hmong village. We knew that the soldiers would not kill, rape, or torture any of us in the presence of other Hmong, because they needed the villagers' loyalty. The pro-communist Hmong treated us like low-class people and made us work like servants, but they also gave us shelter and enough to eat. However, we knew that sooner or later the soldiers would come back and take our men away to the seminar camps.

One day while my husband was out gathering bamboo, he met a man in the forest who asked if he was one of the "new people." Wa told him our story. The man said that some Hmong men would soon come from Thailand to rescue us. "Just act normal, follow orders, and don't try to run away from the village," he said. Wa pretended to start building a house so that the villagers would think we were planning to stay a long time. Meanwhile, I was put to work pounding rice. Pounding rice is boring and time-consuming, but I know how to do it fast, so many families hired me. Each family would give me a little rice after I finished pounding their crop. I worked very hard and, in one month, managed to accumulate a large sack of rice.

One day, four men came to rescue us just as the man in the forest had promised. They were dressed like soldiers and carried guns. They went straight to the village chief and told him that their troops had the village surrounded. Since Hmong New Year was about to begin, they promised the chief that no one would be harmed as long as our group was allowed to leave peacefully. However, if the chief refused to let us

go, the troops would burn every house in the village. Of course it was all a lie, but the chief believed it. That day we walked out of the village with our rescuers, who helped guide us on the journey toward the river. But their service was not free; as our share of the payment, my husband and I had to give them all of the silver we had left.

Some people in our group told my husband to leave his aged mother behind in the village, but he refused to listen. Many of them had already abandoned their elderly parents and grandparents along the way, but Wa had always helped his mother along the trail himself, when no one else would. Now he refused to leave her behind once again, and he also refused to leave the sack of rice that I had worked so hard to earn. I will never forget the sight of him carrying that big sack of rice on his back with Kristie on top of it and his old mother leaning on one arm. I carried most of our dry goods on my back and held Yang in my arms. Song, David, Xeng, and Lo carried baskets on their backs. My husband was the slowest one in our group.

By now there were so many Hmong families trying to get out of the country that the trails were full. We saw the same people day after day and our kids became friends with their kids. Sometimes their play-mates died along the way, a fact of life they had already gotten used to. When we got separated from each other, we used a relay system to send messages from person to person along the trail, as all refugee families did. Even though David and Xeng were small for their ages—nine and eleven years old—they walked faster than the rest of us. One time they got so far ahead we didn't see them for a couple of days. I knew they would be all right; by now they were practically adults and could take care of themselves. My kids had no choice but to grow up fast.

When we finally reached the Mekong, there were dozens of families waiting to cross over to Thailand, and dozens more arriving every day. The Thai boatmen made a very good business for themselves; they were

SOUL CALLING

Chinese silver bars used by H

charging one hu
boatload of peop
or silver left, my
our group if the
turned us down,
passage. Finally,
silver coins, whi
repay the loan,
bride for his son
   We tried to
told us that our
was traveling by

fence. Two years later, they bulldozed the cemetery to make room for more refugee houses.

   After Yang died, we began to see that life in Ban Vinai was not as good as we thought at first. Because of the overcrowding, hot weather, and unsanitary conditions, many people were sick all the time. Moreover, it was not safe to leave the camp for any reason; people who did were regularly beaten up and robbed. The food that aid workers brought us was often stale or rotten because they collected it from local Thai markets after it had gone unsold for several days. I remember getting awful, smelly seafood every week and trying to cook it with lots of peppers to cover up the bad taste.

   My husband and I finally decided to apply for refugee status so we could go to America. But it was not an easy decision. All we knew about the United States were the stories we heard every day around the camp. Some people said that Americans, who we called *nyav*, liked to cook Hmong people and eat them. Others told us that the sun was much closer to the earth in the United States and people were often burned to death if they went outside during the daytime.

   After we completed the paperwork, it took us four months to get an interview. There was a long line that day and we had just ten minutes to convince the case worker that my husband had really served in the war. The only proof we had was our wedding photo showing Wa in his Royal Lao Army uniform; somehow we had managed to hang on to it through twelve years of war and five more years of hiding in the jungle. It was just a tiny black-and-white photo, faded and wrinkled, but now it was our ticket to freedom. When the day arrived for us to board the bus to the Bangkok airport, we were all given big, heavy coats. We could not imagine why.

   It seemed like we had been on the airplane for days when we finally landed in St. Paul. It was dark out and unbelievably cold. The ground was covered with white as far as we could see in every direction. My kids got into an argument about whether the white stuff was salt or sugar and ran outside the airport to have a closer look. They scooped up handfuls of the mysterious substance and tasted it, even though I had told them not to. The sponsors picked us up and drove us to our new home in a big apartment complex. When we woke up the next morning and looked out the window, the ground was still covered with white and there were no people anywhere.

   Later that day, an older American man and his wife who lived in the apartment next door brought us warm food and an old TV set. They liked our kids and tried to help them learn English by pointing at different things and saying the English words. They were poor people like us, but they shared what they had and I will always remember their kindness. Not everyone was so kind, though. Many times during our early years in Minnesota, people would come up to us and say, "You don't belong here; why don't you go back to your country?"

   It was unbelievably cold that winter, so we just stayed inside for the first three months. It was hard to believe that anyone would build a city in such a cold place. When we looked out the window we hardly ever saw anyone. Gradually, the snow melted and people started coming out. Summer arrived with its amazingly long days and we planted a garden. One evening we were out weeding and picking vegetables when we heard gunfire. I grabbed all of the kids and herded them inside as fast as I could. The gunfire continued for half an hour and then the bombing started. I made all of the kids stay down on the floor. I was so scared I felt sick to my stomach. The fighting went on for hours and finally died down after midnight. The next morning everything seemed normal outside, as if nothing had happened. Nobody had told us about the Fourth of July.

   To this day, I still have nightmares about the war and hiding in the jungle. When my kids ask me to go camping with them, I can't bring

Wa Lor Lee and Yer Lor, Xien Khouang Province, Laos 1963.

myself to go because it makes me think of that time. I will carry these memories with me until the day I die. Nothing will ever make them go away. Not the car or the house or the food or the sofa. We did not come to this country because it is a rich country. We did not even want to come; we had no choice but to come here or spend the rest of our lives in the refugee camp. We were not wanted anywhere. I am happy that my children and grandchildren will have a better life than I did. But I am also worried that so many young Hmong today do not respect their elders and are not learning Hmong language and culture. They think that wisdom is how well you speak English, but I believe that wisdom comes from experience. My greatest fear is that our culture will disappear and our families will fall apart.

REFERENCES

LOST AND FOUND, PAGES 109–111

The following sources informed my portrayal of the Hmong belief system and shamanic ceremony:

1. Conquergood, Dwight, et al. *I Am a Shaman: A Hmong Life Story with Ethnographic Commentary.* Minneapolis: Center for Urban and Regional Affairs, University of Minnesota, 1989.

2. Symonds, Patricia V. *Calling in the Soul: Gender and the Cycle of Life in a Hmong Village.* Seattle: University of Washington Press, 2003.

3. Interviews with Yer Lee are cited below under "Hmong Americans/Yer's Story."

PLAIN OF JARS, PAGES 113–116

1. Hamilton-Merritt, Jane. *Tragic Mountains: The Hmong, the Americans, and the Secret Wars for Laos, 1942–1992.* Bloomington: Indiana University Press, 1993. Rife with inaccuracies and untruths, this book combines a hawkish perspective on the war with a sympathetic account of the Hmong refugee plight after it ended.

2. McCoy, Alfred W. *The Politics of Heroin: CIA Complicity in the Global Drug Trade.* Chicago: Lawrence Hill Books, 1991. McCoy makes a compelling case that Laotian generals, including Vang Pao, were heavily involved in buying opium from hill tribe villagers, processing it into heroin, and selling it globally. He further alleges that Vang Pao used the opium trade and USAID rice to coerce Hmong villagers into fighting for the CIA.

3. Warner, Roger. *Shooting at the Moon: The Story of America's Clandestine War in Laos.* South Royalton, VT: Steerforth Press, 1996. Warner's pro-war account provides detailed, unflinching character portrayals of Vang Pao and the key CIA operatives involved in the Secret War, and scrutinizes the many flaws in the operation. He repeats McCoy's allegations about heroin trafficking by Vang Pao and other Laotian generals, however, he adopts the view that the CIA merely looked the other way, rather than actively participating in drug trafficking.

4. Robbins, Christopher. *The Ravens: Pilots of the Secret War of Laos.* Bangkok: Asia Books, 2000. Robbins also repeats many of McCoy's allegations about CIA involvement in drug trafficking, adding details about the use of Air America planes to move opium to and from Lao heroin processing labs. He seconds the allegation that Vang Pao operated a heroin lab at Long Cheng.

5. McCoy details CIA complicity in the trafficking of Laotian heroin to Vietnam and its impact on American GIs.

6. Hamilton-Merritt makes the case for Hmong cultural opposition to communism.

7. McCoy describes Vang Pao's use of USAID rice drops to control the Hmong villagers. He also gives his own firsthand account of seeing a Hmong village bombed by American planes when Vang Pao feared the inhabitants might switch sides in the wake of the Hmong retreat.

8. Hamilton-Merritt and Warner offer widely varying descriptions of Vang Pao's evacuation from Long Cheng. Warner provides considerable detail on the seven wives.

9. *Khao Xane Pathet Lao* (Lao People's Party daily newspaper), Vientiane, May 9, 1975: "…the Hmong people must be exterminated to the root."

10. Long, Lynellen. *Ban Vinai: The Refugee Camp.* New York: Columbia University Press, 1993. The author provides an account of life in the largest of the Hmong refugee camps, including many refugee narratives.

11. Hamilton-Merritt is the primary proponent of the allegation that Russian-made chemical weapons ("yellow rain") were sprayed on Hmong villages from the air after 1975. However, neither the UNHCR nor any major human rights organizations have ever confirmed this allegation. Nevertheless, her case is compelling and many eyewitnesses have supported it. A Fresno medical clinic serving Southeast Asian patients has wall placards describing yellow rain symptoms.

12. Kittavong Amarathidatha, a Lao refugee, interviewed by Joel Pickford, Madison, Wisconsin, July 2007: "… fleeing the tiger to meet the lion."

13. Accounts of Hmong refugees being robbed by Thai soldiers and police are found in Hamilton-Merritt, Long, and in my interviews with the Lee family cited in the notes for "Yer Lor Lee" (p. 253). There are also many accounts of Thai soldiers helping the refugees who crossed the river in the early years of the exodus, however, as the years passed and the numbers of Hmong refugees increased, the Thai soldiers became more jaded and increasingly began to see them only as a source of illicit income.

14. Warner interviewed Bill Lair, the architect of the Secret War, at length; he is the central character of Warner's book. Lair admits that he thought the operation was unlikely to succeed and describes a plan he developed early on to relocate future Hmong refugees to Sainyabouri Province in Laos, southwest of the Mekong River, where he thought they would be safe from persecution.

15. Hamilton-Merritt describes the incident in which half the soldiers in a Hmong unit—roughly fifty men and boys—died rescuing a single American pilot who had been shot down behind enemy lines.

16. Kamm, Henry. "Decades-Old U.S. Bombs Still Killing Laotians." *New York Times*, August 10, 1995.

17. *Bombies*. Documentary film about the lingering effects of UXO from the American bombing of Laos, directed by Jack Silberman, Lumiere Productions for ITVS-PBS, 2002.

18. Mines Advisory Group (MAG) website for Lao operations, http://www.maginternational.org/MAG/en/news/lao-pdr-updates/. The Mines Advisory Group is a neutral and impartial humanitarian organization clearing the remnants of conflict for the benefit of communities worldwide. The page has links to articles by MAG staff writers that provide additional statistics about the United States' bombing of Laos and its present-day aftermath.

NEW ARRIVALS, PAGES 117–119

The saga of the Hovannisian family and JD Home Rentals, Inc., is based on the following newspaper articles and interviews:

1. Pulaski, Alex. "Despair and Disrepair: Tenants Say They Are Victims of an Uncaring Landlord." *Fresno Bee*, March 10, 1991.

2. Dudley, Anne. "Lung Wants 'Slum' Owners Out of Apartment Business." *Fresno Bee*, September 22, 1993.

3. Coyne, Eric. "City's 'Worst' Dwellings Get Lung's Wrath." *Fresno Bee*, October 1, 1993.

4. Fontana, Cyndee. "Ex, Current Tenants Sue Rental Company: Suit Against JD Home Rentals of Fresno Alleges Substandard Conditions." *Fresno Bee*, October 3, 1997.

5. Bruner, Karla. "Plaintiffs Cite Unsafe Conditions in Rentals: Lawsuit Says Defects Were Not Repaired Despite Repeated Requests." *Fresno Bee*, October 3, 1997.

6. Fontana, Cyndee. "Suit Spurs Calls Against Rental Firm: Valley Landlord Faces Complaint from 112 Current and Former Tenants." *Fresno Bee*, October 4, 1997.

7. Yoshino, Kim. "Pop Team Sponsors Meeting of Landlords: Owners, Managers of Southeast Fresno Apartments Discuss Problem-Tenant Options." *Fresno Bee*, March 12, 1998.

8. Krikorian, Michael. "From Armenia with Love: Family Members Gather to Celebrate Siroon Hovannisian's 90th Birthday in Fresno." *Fresno Bee*, January 10, 2000.

9. Arax, Mark, and Rick Wartzman. *The King of California: J. G. Boswell and the Making of a Secret American Empire*. New York: Public Affairs, 2003. The authors describe Kaspar Hovannisian's early years as a real estate investor buying highway houses and renting them to black sharecroppers and Mexican braceros.

10. Kim Thompson, meetings with Joel Pickford, Fresno, California, February and March 2005. Thompson is the former director of the housing program for Fresno Interdenominational Refugee Ministries (FIRM). In the meetings, she described many specific code violations and code enforcement issues related to JD Home Rentals properties and the efforts of her program to assist Hmong and other refugee tenants through legal action. She also cited the more than $250,000 spent by Fresno County Code Enforcement in 2004 solely to address complaints about Hovannisian properties.

11. JoJo Mosesian, interviewed by Joel Pickford, Fresno, California, October 12, 2009. A friend of David Hovannisian and fellow car enthusiast, Mosesian describes Hovannisian's collection of cars and other collectibles.

TOUT TOU, PAGES 121–122

1. Xiong, Blong, ed. "Journey to Freedom: The Hmong Resettlement Task Force Report from Wat Tham Krabok, April 19–23, 2004." Fresno: Center for New Americans, 2004.

2. Tout Tou Bounthapanya, interviewed by Joel Pickford, Fresno, California, March 2005.

POLYGAMY, PAGES 127–130

1. Ka Vang (pseudonym), interviewed by Tout Tou Bounthapanya and Joel Pickford, April 2005, and again by Tess Nealy and Tout Tou Bounthapanya on May 11, 2005. Ka's descriptions of and opinions about polygamous marriage are drawn from these two interviews.

2. Warner gives a remarkably similar description of how General Vang Pao and his six wives organized their household at Long Cheng.

JU CHA, PAGES 131–135

1. De Lollis, Barbara. "Promises Broken." *Fresno Bee*, March 3, 1997. The article details the history of Valley Children's Hospital's move from Central Fresno to southern Madera County after developer Richard Gunner lured the hospital's board by donating the land.

2. Anderson, Barbara, and Correa, Tracy. "Valley Children's Fires 51." *Fresno Bee*, July 22, 2000. The article reports the hospital's drastic staff cuts after the move to the remote rural location resulted in a major loss of patients and revenue. The CEO who presided over the move, J. D. Northway, retired just prior to the firings.

3. Correa, Tracy. "Developer Works on Area Near Children's Hospital in Madera, Calif." *Fresno Bee*, July 13, 2003. The article details developer Richard Gunner's stalled plans to sprawl a new city on the farmland surrounding the hospital.

4. McCarthy, Charles. "Board Demands VCH Fee: Madera County Denies Hospital's Appeal of $389,144 Bill for Road Improvement Costs." *Fresno Bee*. The article reports on the final resolution disputes over Highway 41 bridge expansion costs caused by the building of the hospital on the remote San Joaquin River bluffs.

5. Delcore, Henry. "In Praise of an Unheralded Hero." Op-ed column, *Fresno Bee*, September 16, 2006. This column describes the life and funeral of clan leader Hlaw Lee.

IMPROVISATION, PAGES 137–143

1. The Lee family interviews are cited under "Yer Lor Lee," on p. 253. The story of the high school student who was frightened by her vision of a dragon in Huntington Lake was told to me by Yer Lee, who performed ceremonies to help her. Kristie Lee's biographical sketch is also drawn from these interviews.

2. My statement about the decline in young Hmong brides being treated like indentured servants by their husbands' families in the United States but still occurring in Laos is based on my own observations in both countries as well as anecdotal information from Hmong informants; statistical information on this topic would be impossible to obtain.

HMONG AMERICANS, PAGES 145–148

1. Long describes how narrative *pab ntaub*, or "story cloths," first originated in the refugee camps through the encouragement of missionaries and as a way to earn income. Prior to the war, only traditional abstract designs were used in Hmong *pab ntaub* embroidery in Laos and China.

LIFE AND DEATH IN A HMONG VILLAGE, PAGES 221–225

1. My descriptions of the funeral and references to the Hmong cosmology are informed by Conquergood, Symonds, and my interviews with the Lee family.

XYOO TSHIAB/NEW YEAR, PAGES 227–238

Though mainly based on my own observations, my understanding of Hmong New Year is also informed by the following sources:

1. Cooper, Robert, ed. *The Hmong: A Guide to Traditional Lifestyles: Vanishing Cultures of the World*. Singapore: Times Editions, 1998.

2. Downing, Bruce T., and Douglas P. Olney, eds. *The Hmong in the West: Observations and Reports*. Minneapolis: Center for Urban and Regional Affairs, 1982.

3. Geddes, William R. *Migrants of the Mountains: The Cultural Ecology of the Blue Miao (Hmong Njua) of Thailand*. Oxford, UK: Clarendon Press, 1976.

4. Warner and Robbins both discuss the strategic importance of Xam Neua Province during the war and the differing allegiances of the clans and villages, which were less unified than their counterparts in Xieng Khouang Province.

YER LOR LEE, PAGES 239–249

My description of the Lee family and Yer's personal story are based on numerous visits to their homes and the following transcribed interviews:

REFERENCES

1. Yer Lor Lee and translator David Lee, interviewed by Dr. Henry Delcore and project intern Tess Nealy, February 27, 2006. This interview covers some parts of Yer's refugee narrative and becoming a shaman.

2. Yer Lor Lee, Wa Lor Lee, and translator David Lee, interviewed by Joel Pickford, April 2, 2006. The refugee narrative continues.

3. Yer Lor Lee, interviewed and translated by Ue Yang, July 2008. This interview focuses on shamanic practice and its underlying cosmological beliefs.

4. Yer Lor Lee and translator David Lee, interviewed by Joel Pickford, September 1, 2008. This interview focuses on Yer's childhood and parents; early village life; her mother and aunt's shamanic practice; becoming a shaman; examples of shamanic client cases; her early memories of the Secret War, American soldiers, and Vang Pao; additional parts of her refugee narrative; and arriving in the United States.

5. Wa Lor Lee and translator David Lee, interviewed by Joel Pickford, October 28, 2008. This interview focuses on Wa's early childhood, village life, and military training and career.

6. Yer Lor Lee, Wa Lor Lee, and translator David Lee, interviewed by Joel Pickford, November 15, 2008. This interview focuses on life in Ban Vinai refugee camp.

7. Hamilton-Merritt describes the Hmong massacre at Hin Heup Bridge near Vang Vieng, Laos. Hamilton-Merritt and other sources, such as Warner, Robbins, and Fadiman, proffer widely varying casualty figures, ranging from several dozen to ten thousand.

BIBLIOGRAPHY

Adler, Shelley Ruth. *The Role of the Nightmare in Hmong Sudden Unexpected Nocturnal Death Syndrome: A Folkloristic Study of Belief and Health.* PhD thesis, University of California, Los Angeles, 1991.

Agee, James, and Walker Evans. *Let Us Now Praise Famous Men: Three Tenant Families.* Boston: Houghton Mifflin, 1960. (First published in 1939.)

Alisa, Karin, ed. *The Hmong.* Detroit: Greenhaven Press, 2007.

Arax, Mark, and Rick Wartzman. *The King of California: J. G. Boswell and the Making of a Secret American Empire.* New York: Public Affairs, 2003.

Arbus, Diane. *Diane Arbus: Revelations.* New York: Random House, 2003.

Between Two Worlds: A Hmong Shaman in America. Documentary film produced by Taggart Siegel and Dwight Conquergood, Filmmakers Library, New York, 2001.

Bliatout, Bruce Thowpaou. *Hmong Sudden Unexpected Nocturnal Death Syndrome: A Cultural Study.* Portland, OR: Sparkle Publishing, 1982.

Bombies. Documentary film about the lingering effects of UXO from the American bombing of Laos, directed by Jack Silberman, Lumiere Productions for ITVS-PBS, 2002.

Bosworth, Patricia. *Diane Arbus: A Biography.* New York: Knopf, 1984.

Catlin, Amy, and Dixie Swift, eds. *Textiles as Texts: Arts of Hmong Women from Laos.* Los Angeles: The Women's Building, 1987.

Conquergood, Dwight, et al. *I Am a Shaman: A Hmong Life Story with Ethnographic Commentary.* Minneapolis: Center for Urban and Regional Affairs, University of Minnesota, 1989.

Cooper, Robert, ed. *The Hmong: A Guide to Traditional Lifestyles: Vanishing Cultures of the World.* Singapore: Times Editions, 1998.

Cummings, Joe, and Andrew Burke. *Lonely Planet Laos.* Oakland, CA: Lonely Planet Publications, 2004.

Dao, Yang. *Hmong at the Turning Point.* Minneapolis: WorldBridge Associates, 1993.

Downing, Bruce T., and Douglas P. Olney, eds. *The Hmong in the West: Observations and Reports.* Minneapolis: Center for Urban and Regional Affairs, 1982.

Evans, Grant. *A Short History of Laos: The Land In Between.* New South Wales, Australia: Allen and Unwin, 2002.

Faderman, Lillian, with Ghia Xiong. *I Begin My Life All Over: The Hmong and the American Immigrant Experience.* Boston: Beacon Press, 1998.

Fadiman, Anne. *The Spirit Catches You and You Fall Down: A Hmong Child, Her American Doctors, and the Collision of Two Cultures.* New York: Farrar, Straus and Giroux, 1998.

Frank, Robert, and Sarah Greenough. *Looking In: Robert Frank's Americans, Expanded Edition.* Washington, DC: National Gallery of Art/Steidl, 2009.

Frank, Robert, and Jack Kerouac. *The Americans.* New York: Grossman, 1969. (First published in France as *Les Americains,* 1958.)

Geddes, William R. *Migrants of the Mountains: The Cultural Ecology of the Blue Miao (Hmong Njua) of Thailand.* Oxford, UK: Clarendon Press, 1976.

Guns, Drugs, and the CIA. "PBS Frontline" documentary produced by Leslie and Andrew Cockburn, broadcast May 17, 1988.

Hamilton-Merritt, Jane. *Tragic Mountains: The Hmong, The Americans, and the Secret Wars for Laos, 1942–1992.* Bloomington: Indiana University Press, 1993.

Herr, Michael. *Dispatches.* New York: Alfred A. Knopf, 1977.

Johns, Brenda, and David Strecker, eds. *The Hmong World.* New Haven, CT: Yale University, Southeast Asia Studies, 1986.

Johnson, Charles, ed. *Dab Neeb Hmoob: Myths, Legends, and Folk Tales from the Hmong of Laos.* Written and translated by Se Yang, et al. St. Paul, MN: Macalester College, 1985.

Lederer, William J., and Burdick, Eugene. *The Ugly American*. New York: Norton, 1958.

Livo, Norma J., and Dia Cha, eds. *Folk Stories of the Hmong: Peoples of Laos, Thailand, and Vietnam*. Englewood, CO: Libraries Unlimited, 1991.

Long, Lynellen. *Ban Vinai: The Refugee Camp*. New York: Columbia University Press, 1993.

McCoy, Alfred W. *The Politics of Heroin: CIA Complicity in the Global Drug Trade*. Chicago: Lawrence Hill Books, 1991.

Menger, Matt J. *In the Valley of the Mekong: An American in Laos*. Paterson, NJ: St. Anthony Guild Press, 1970.

Mottin, Jean. *The History of the Hmong*. Bangkok: Odeon Store, 1980.

Moua, Mai Neng. *Bamboo Among the Oaks: Contemporary Writing by Hmong Americans*. St. Paul: Minnesota Historical Society Press, 2002.

Quincy, Keith. *Hmong: History of a People*. Cheney, WA: Eastern Washington University Press, 1988.

Rathbone, Belinda. *Walker Evans: A Biography*. Boston: Houghton Mifflin, 1995.

Robbins, Christopher. *The Ravens: Pilots of the Secret War of Laos*. Bangkok: Asia Books, 2000.

Stuart-Fox, Martin. *A History of Laos*. Cambridge, UK: Cambridge University Press, 1997.

Symonds, Patricia V. *Calling in the Soul: Gender and the Cycle of Life in a Hmong Village*. Seattle: University of Washington Press, 2003.

Tapp, Nicholas. *The Hmong of Thailand: Opium People of the Golden Triangle*. London: Anti-Slavery Society, and Cambridge, MA: Cultural Survival Inc., 1986.

Tapp, Nicholas. *The Hmong of China: Context, Agency, and the Imaginary*. Leiden, Netherlands: Brill, 2001.

Tapp, Nicholas, Jean Michaud, Christian Culas, and Gary Yia Lee, eds. *Hmong-Miao in Asia*. Chiang Mai, Thailand: Silkworm Books, 2004.

Theroux, Paul. *The Great Railway Bazaar: By Train Through Asia*. Boston: Houghton Mifflin, 1975.

Vang, Burlee, ed. *New Threads: A Chapbook of Writing and Poetry from Hmong Americans*. A project of the Hmong American Writers' Circle. Fresno: Stone Soup Fresno, 2008.

Warner, Roger. *Shooting at the Moon: The Story of America's Clandestine War in Laos*. South Royalton, VT: Steerforth Press, 1996.

Xiong, Blong, ed. "Journey to Freedom: The Hmong Resettlement Task Force Report from Wat Tham Krabok, April 19–23, 2004." Fresno: Center for New Americans, 2004.

Yang, Kao Kalia. *The Latehomecomer: A Hmong Family Memoir*. Minneapolis: Coffee House Press, 2008.

PROJECT TEAM MEMBERS

Joel Pickford, photographer and writer
Dr. Henry Delcore, project advisor and professor of anthropology at California State University, Fresno (CSUF)
Tout Tou Bounthapanya, trilingual interpreter and social worker
Kristie Lee, bilingual interpreter and social worker
David Lee, bilingual interpreter and teacher
Yer Lor Lee, Hmong master shaman and project advisor
Neng Thao Lee, Hmong clan leader and project advisor
Paula Yang, bilingual interpreter and Hmong community activist
Wayne Vang, trilingual interpreter and Hmong community activist
Kim Thompson, former housing project director for Fresno Interdenominational Refugee Ministries (FIRM)
Long Vang, trilingual interpreter and guide, Xieng Khouang Province, Laos
Toua Moua, trilingual interpreter and guide, Luang Prabang Province, Laos
Toua Her, CSUF student intern
Tess Neely, CSUF student intern
Challencen Vang, CSUF student intern

GRADUATE THESIS COMMITTEE

Prof. Steven Church, Chair
Dr. Henry Delcore
Dr. Lillian Faderman

PROJECT PARTNER ORGANIZATIONS

California Council for the Humanities, California Stories Initiative, funding partner
The James Irvine Foundation, funding partner
Fresno Historical Society, Jill Moffat, Executive Director
Fresno Interdenominational Refugee Ministries, Rev. Sharon Stanley, Executive Director

CAPTIONS

THE NEW ARRIVALS, 2004–2006

"New Arrivals" title page: Mai Kou Yang and her children on their second day in America, Fresno, 2005.

Plate 1   Xiong siblings, Fue Houa, Jong, Mai Ju, and Vu, after their first week in Fresno, 2005.

Plate 2   Jong Xiong is one of three blind children in his family of eleven, Fresno, 2005.

Plate 3   New arrivals at the Fresno Yosemite International Airport, 2005.

Plate 4   Hmong apartment complex after a recent fire, Clovis, 2007.

Plate 5   Refugee apartment complex, Southeast Fresno, 2005.

Plate 6   Hmong boy playing near a dumpster, Southeast Fresno, 2005.

Plate 7   Fenced-in drainage basin (a code violation), near Fresno Fairgrounds, 2005.

Plate 8   Thirty-four members of the Vang family (pseudonym) share a four-bedroom house, Fresno, 2005.

Plate 9   Thong Vang eats alone in his family's kitchen, Fresno, 2005.

Plate 10   Hmong apartment front porch, Southeast Fresno, 2005.

Plate 11   Dia Lor, Fresno, 2005.

Plate 12   Hmong apartment vegetable garden, Southeast Fresno, 2005.

Plate 13   New-arrival grandmother holds her grandson, Tou Vang, Fresno, 2005.

Plate 14   Arriving in December, Nou Teng Her and his wife are not yet accustomed to winter in central California, Fresno, 2005.

Plate 15   After arriving from Wat Tham Krabok, the family of Mai Ku Yang still stores water in jugs and eats Lao-style, Fresno, 2005.

Plate 16   Lang Thao has no toys to play with and nothing to do, Fresno, 2005.

Plate 17   Recent arrival Va Ser Chang, 99, on the back porch of his new home, Fresno, 2005.

Plate 18   Yee Chang in the kitchen where she burnt a skillet full of hot peppers, Fresno, 2005.

Plate 19   A deaf couple, Chia Thao and his wife, with their children after one week in a Fresno apartment complex, 2005.

Plate 20   Detail of the Thao family photo collage, Fresno 2005.

Plate 21   Fa Lue Thao, 102, is one of the last refugees to arrive, Merced, 2006.

Plate 22   Tai Her, 17, and her son, Bee Lee, Fresno, 2005.

Plate 23   Luke Thao gazes at tadpoles caught in the canal behind his apartment complex, Fresno, 2005.

Plate 24   Kong Cheng Thao and Lang Thao have nothing to do so they act out, Fresno, 2005.

Plate 25   Pregnant Ka Vue (pseudonym) gets ready for Hmong New Year, Fresno, 2005.

Plate 26   Toua Moua Vang and his two wives, Ka Vue and Mai Moua (pseudonyms), Fresno, 2005.

Plate 27   Ka Vue nurses her newborn baby, Fresno, 2005.

Plate 28   Ju Cha and her four-year-old son, Fresno, 2005.

Plate 29   Ju Cha feeds her premature baby on the back porch, Fresno, 2005.

Plate 30   Ju Cha's baby at one month, Fresno, 2005.

Plate 31   Cher Ker Thao and his wife in front of their new home, Clovis, 2005.

Plate 32   Shamanic altar, Clovis, 2005.

Plate 33   Teng Xiong holds his great-niece, Fresno, 2006. Two months later he took his own life.

Plate 34   Nou Thao is growing up in two cultures, Clovis, 2005.

HMONG AMERICANS

"Hmong Americans" title page: Shaman Chee Yang performs a *ua neeb* ceremony using a dead pig and a twelve-pack of Pepsi as offerings, Fresno, 2005.

Plate 35   Deaf musician Wa Yee Vang plays his homemade flute with a medicine bottle attached, Clovis, 2005.

Plate 36   Wa Yee Vang at a neighbor's apartment, Clovis, 2005.

Plate 37   A rare red-hood shaman performs a *ua neeb* ceremony, Clovis, 2006.

Plate 38   Chee Yang performs a *ua neeb* for fellow shaman Yer Lor Lee, Fresno, 2006.

Plate 39   Yer Lor Lee burns spirit money, Fresno, 2005.

Plate 40   Wa Lor Lee beats the gong to accompany his wife's spirit trance. The wooden bench represents a horse that she rides into the spirit world. Fresno, 2005.

Plate 41   Shaman Yer Lor Lee calls the soul from the back door of her home, Fresno, 2005.

Plate 42   Wa Lor Lee steadies his wife as she leaps on and off the bench, Fresno, 2005.

Plate 43   Soul calling ceremony for Wang Thao Vang and his wife, Ge Xiong, Fresno, 2005.

Plate 44   Yer Lor Lee bids her sister-in-law farewell before she and Yer's brother, Ga Pao Lor, return to Laos from Fresno, 2005.

Plate 45   The men eat first after a soul calling ceremony, Fresno, 2005.

Plate 46   Hmong cooking always uses fresh ingredients.

Plate 47   Xiong Pao Her holds a snap pea pod, Sanger, 2008.

Plate 48   Ker Yang looks over his land southeast of Fresno, 2005.

Plate 49   Xiong Pao Her checks his irrigation system, Sanger, 2008.

Plate 50   Mee Moua harvests long beans, Sanger, 2008.

Plate 51   Chong Yang gets ready to drive a truckload of strawberries to the broker, Merced, 2006.

Plate 52   Hmong farmers grow Asian specialty crops in hothouses, Sanger, 2008.

Plate 53   Ye Lor wears typical homemade clothing for protection from the sun while working in his fields, southeastern Fresno County, 2008.

Plate 54   Ye Lor's wife harvests spinach from her family farm, southeastern Fresno County, 2008.

Plate 55   Freshly picked strawberries from Ge Paul Yang's farm, Merced, 2006.

Plate 56   The last strawberry harvest for Ge Paul Yang and his wife, Mai Ying Moua, Merced, 2006.

Plate 57   Friends and relatives of the Yang family gather the day after their mobile home caught fire, killing three, Clovis, 2006.

Plate 58   Alyssa Yang returns to the scene where two of her older sisters and her uncle died a month earlier, Clovis, 2006.

Plate 59   Tommy Her and friends mourn the loss of schoolmates Ia and Pakou Yang, Clovis, 2006.

Plate 60   Roxane Moua and Eve Cha light a candle in memory of their friends Ia and Pakou Yang, who died in the fire, Clovis, 2006.

Plate 61   Candlelight vigils for the Yang family continued for five nights at the site of the mobile home fire, Clovis, 2006.

Plate 62   A relative comforts Doua Yang, mother of the two teenage girls who died in the fire, Clovis, 2006.

Plate 63   Family members mourn the loss of Ia Yang, Fresno, 2006.

Plate 64   Funeral for Pakou Yang, victim of the mobile home fire, Fresno, 2006.

Plate 65   Vicki Cha grieves for her lost boyfriend, Shee Yang, Fresno, 2006.

Plate 66   Hearse with photograph of Shee Yang, Fresno, 2006.

Plate 67   Chong Yang (with arm in sling) watches as his younger brother Shee's casket is buried, Fresno, 2006.

Plate 68   May Yang holds a photograph of her younger sister Pakou as she watches the burial, Fresno, 2006.

Plate 69   Shee Yang's shoes are buried with his casket, Fresno, 2006.

Plate 70   Chong Yang watches as his daughter Pakou's casket is placed in the grave, Fresno, 2006.

Plate 71   Funeral for Neng Yia Lo, Fresno, 2008.

Plate 72   *Qeej* player at the funeral for Hlaw Neng Thao Lee, Fresno, 2006.

Plate 73   Members of the Lee family honor their fallen clan leader, Hlaw Neng, Fresno, 2006.

Plate 74   Xe Lee pays respects to Hlaw Neng, Fresno, 2006.

Plate 75   Chue Doua Herr surrounded by his wife, daughter, and many clan members, Clovis, 2007. In 1975, Major Herr was the last commander in the Royal Lao Army to defend Vientiane before it fell to the communists.

Plate 76   Funeral drum, Clovis, 2007.

Plate 77   Vang Nou grieves for her husband, Chue Doua Herr, at his burial, Fresno, 2007.

Plate 78   Clan members make spirit money offerings to pay the soul's way back home to Laos, Clovis, 2007. On the final day of the funeral, all of the spirit money will be gathered up and burned.

Plate 79   Neng Lee plays the *qeej* at the funeral for Chue Doua Herr, Clovis, 2007.

Plate 80   Herr family elders seated around the pig that is traditionally offered to the spirits at Hmong funerals, Clovis, 2007.

Plate 81   Yong Khue Herr, brother, and Zang Herr, grandson, at the burial for Chue Doua Herr, Fresno, 2007.

Plate 82   Men of the Herr clan hold an all-night vigil at the funeral for their leader, Chue Doua Herr, Clovis, 2007.

Plate 83   Sugarcane vendor at Fresno Hmong New Year, 2004.

Plate 84   A member of the Xiong clan seated in front of a portrait photography backdrop showing the 1975 evacuation of Long Cheng, Fresno Hmong New Year, 2005.

Plate 85   Octogenarian at the Fresno Hmong New Year, 2004.

Plate 86   Chao Yang wears money bags laden with old French coins, Fresno Hmong New Year, 2004.

Plate 87   Pob Tsuas Her wears traditional metalwork, Fresno Hmong New Year, 2005.

Plate 88   Girl wearing Chinese-style hat with hanging beads, Fresno Hmong New Year, 2004.

Plate 89   Widows and widowers playing *pov pob*, the tradional Hmong courtship game, in the hope of finding new spouses, Fresno Hmong New Year, 2004.

Plate 90   Eligible young women toss the ball, Fresno Hmong New Year, 2004.

Plate 91   Girl wearing a contemporary update of the Flowered Hmong tribal costume, Fresno Hmong New Year, 2005.

Plate 92   Girl wearing a contemporary costume with a mixture of Yao and Hmong design motifs. (The Yao are a distinct Southeast Asian hill tribe people, a few of whom fought alongside the Hmong in the Secret War.) Fresno Hmong New Year, 2004.

Plate 93   Hmong movies, Fresno Hmong New Year, 2005.

Plate 94   Amateur videographers at Fresno Hmong New Year, 2004.

Plate 95   "Hmong Hotties" calendar and video vendors, Fresno Hmong New Year, 2004.

Plate 96   Woman in Xieng Khouang–style costume poses in front of a backdrop showing the CIA landing field at Long Cheng, Fresno Hmong New Year, 2004.

Plate 97   Wa Lor Lee holds a photo of his special guerilla unit during the Secret War, Fresno, 2005.

Plate 98   Hmong veteran Va Xeng Thao at Fresno Refugee Recognition Day, Fresno Fairgrounds, 2005.

Plate 99   Peter Vang Chou and his wife, May Yang, at a celebration honoring the fortieth anniversary of his career as the first Hmong pilot in the Secret War, Atwater, 2006.

Plate 100   A member of the Vang clan who lost an eye in the Secret War, at an event organized to honor Hmong Veterans, Clovis, 2008.

Plate 101   General Vang Pao and his bodyguards, Fresno, 2009.

Plate 102   Followers of Vang Pao at a rally protesting his imprisonment on charges of plotting to overthrow the Lao government, Fresno County Courthouse, 2007.

Plate 103   A series of rallies protesting Vang Pao's jailing were held at the Fresno and Sacramento County Courthouses, 2007.

Plate 104   General Vang Pao on parole, awaiting trial, Fresno, 2009.

HMONG VILLAGE LIFE IN LAOS

"Hmong Village Life in Laos" title page: Rice paddies, Xieng Khouang Province, 2006.

Plate 105   Hmong woman with her grandson, Luang Prabang Province, 2006.

Plate 106   Hmong girl caries her little brother along a path surrounded by typical Luang Prabang–style bamboo houses, 2006.

Plate 107   Woman in Black Hmong tribal costume, Luang Prabang Province, 2006.

Plate 108   Hmong girl takes care of her brother while her mother pounds rice, Luang Prabang Province, 2006.

Plate 109   Hmong musician plays the *nkauj nog ncas*, a traditional string instrument, made from a rusting can, Vientiane Province, 2007.

Plate 110   Xieng Khouang–style house with loft, Ban Tha Chok, 2006.

Plate 111   Hmong elder, Luang Prabang Province, 2006.

Plate 112   Child eating rice in front of the year's bagged harvest, Luang Prabang Province, 2006.

Plate 113   Hmong house, Ban Kiewtaolaosoung, Luang Prabang Province, 2011.

Plate 114   Hmong mother of nine with her youngest child, Ban Keiwtaolaosoung, Luang Prabang Province, 2011.

Plate 115   Traditional Hmong hearth, Ban Kheopatou, Xieng Khouang Province, 2007.

Plate 116   Vegetable garden, Ban Tha Chok, Xieng Khouang Province, 2006.

Plate 117   Child and dog, Ban Kiewtaolaosoung, Luang Prabang Province, 2011.

Plate 118   Village elder, Ban Kiewtaolaosoung, Luang Prabang Province, 2011.

Plate 119   Baby sleeping on a traditional Hmong palette, Luang Prabang Province, 2006.

Plate 120   Mountain village girl, Luang Prabang Province, 2006.

Plate 121   Village Elder, Ban Pha Keo, Xieng Khouang Province, 2007.

Plate 122   Ban Pha Keo village, Xieng Khouang Province, 2007.

Plate 123   Children play with a toy purchased from itinerant Chinese traders, Ban Tha Chok, Xieng Khouang Province, 2006.

Plate 124   Schoolhouse without electricity, Ban Pha Keo, Xieng Khouang Province, 2007.

Plate 125   Pig destined to be sacrificed for a *ua neeb* ceremony, Luang Prabang Province, 2006.

Plate 126   A shaman calling the soul from the back door, Luang Prabang Province, 2006.

Plate 127   A shaman performs a *ua neeb* ceremony for Toua Moua, Luang Prabang Province, 2006.

Plate 128   A pig is killed on the floor of the house for a *ua neeb* ceremony, Luang Prabang Province, 2006.

Plate 129   A *qeej* player and drummer perform at a funeral as spirit money burns, Ban Tha Chok, Xieng Khouang Province, 2006.

Plate 130   Nee Vang, 24, mourns the death of her seventh child, Ban Tha Chok, Xieng Khouang Province, 2006.

Plate 131   Nee Vang and her sister share the responsibility of mourning the deceased infant, Ban Tha Chok, Xieng Khouang Province, 2006.

Plate 132   Funeral mourners caress the body of a deceased infant, Ban Tha Chok, Xieng Khouang Province, 2006.

Plate 133   Drunken man claiming to be a CIA operative, outside a funeral, Ban Tha Chok, Xieng Khouang Province, 2006.

Plate 134   Plain of Jars, Xieng Khouang Province, 2006.

Plate 135   American bomb shell casings, Ban Tha Chok, Xieng Khouang Province, 2007.

Plate 136   Bomb crater near Ban Tha Chok, Xieng Khouang Province, 2007.

Plate 137   Hmong boys play with a bomb casing, Xam Neua, 2006.

Plate 138   Corn grinding apparatus made from wood, rope, stone, and war scrap; fence made from bomb casings in background, Ban Tha Chok, Xieng Khouang Province, 2006.

Plate 139   A woman and child rest during the rice harvest, Nong Het District, Xieng Khouang Province, 2007.

Plate 140 Slash-and-burn agriculture makes rice farming possible on near-vertical mountainsides, Luang Prabang Province, 2006.

Plate 141 An eighteen-year-old mother takes a break from cutting rice stalks, sitting on a charred tree trunk to keep her balance, Xieng Khouang Province, 2007.

Plate 142 Children of the fields, Nong Het District, Xieng Khouang Province, 2007.

Plate 143 Child sleeping on spent rice stalks, Xieng Khouang Province, 2007.

Plate 144 Scythe used for harvesting rice, Xieng Khouang Province, 2007.

Plate 145 Hmong women sew new costumes every New Year, Luang Prabang Province, 2006.

Plate 146 Hmong children celebrate New Year, Vang Vieng Valley, 2006.

Plate 147 Black Hmong villagers show off superior ball-tossing skills, Xam Neua, 2006.

Plate 148 White Hmong toss homemade balls, Xam Neua, 2006.

Plate 149 A shaman goes from house to house performing soul calling ceremonies for New Year, Xam Neua, 2006.

Plate 150 A red-hood shaman performs a New Year soul calling ceremony, Xam Neua, 2006.

Plate 151 Hmong fighting bulls have been bred for centuries, Xam Neua, 2006.

Plate 152 Hmong bullfights draw large crowds near the Plain of Jars, Xieng Khouang Province, 2006.

Plate 153 Hmong fighting bulls square off in Ban Nong Oun, Xam Neua, 2006.

Plate 154 Water buffalo bulls make much more formidable opponents than Hmong bulls, Xam Neua, 2006.

Plate 155 Hillside village, Xam Neua, 2006.

Plate 156 A Hmong man performing a New Year soul calling ceremony in his own home, Xam Neua, 2006.

Plate 157 A Hmong woman mourns the loss of her twenty-one-year-old daughter at a funeral, Ban Long Ang, Xam Neua, 2006.

Plate 158 Hmong families in Ban Long Ang keep fires burning around the clock to stay warm, Xam Neua, 2006.

Plate 159 Man in traditional black village clothing, Ban Long Ang, Xam Neua, 2006.

Plate 160 Woman wearing heirloom silver and copper neck pieces, Xam Neua, 2006.

Plate 161 Hmong Boy wearing a talisman to ward off the bad spirits that cause illness, Ban Long Ang, Xam Neua, 2006.

Plate 162 In the morning mist, the mountains of Xam Neua evoke Ntuj Khiab Haub, the mythical Hmong homeland, 2006.